TEMPLES OF JUSTICE

WILBUR S. SHEPPERSON SERIES IN HISTORY & HUMANITIES

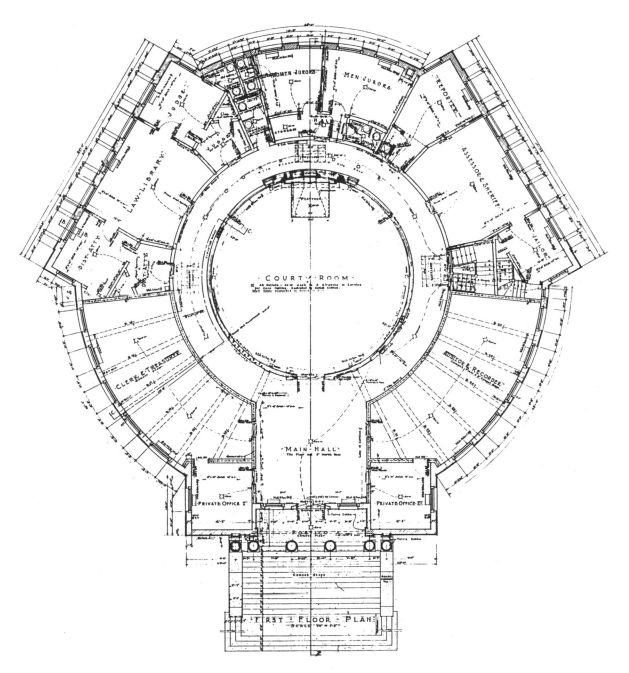

RONALD M. JAMES

FOREWORD BY CLIFF YOUNG

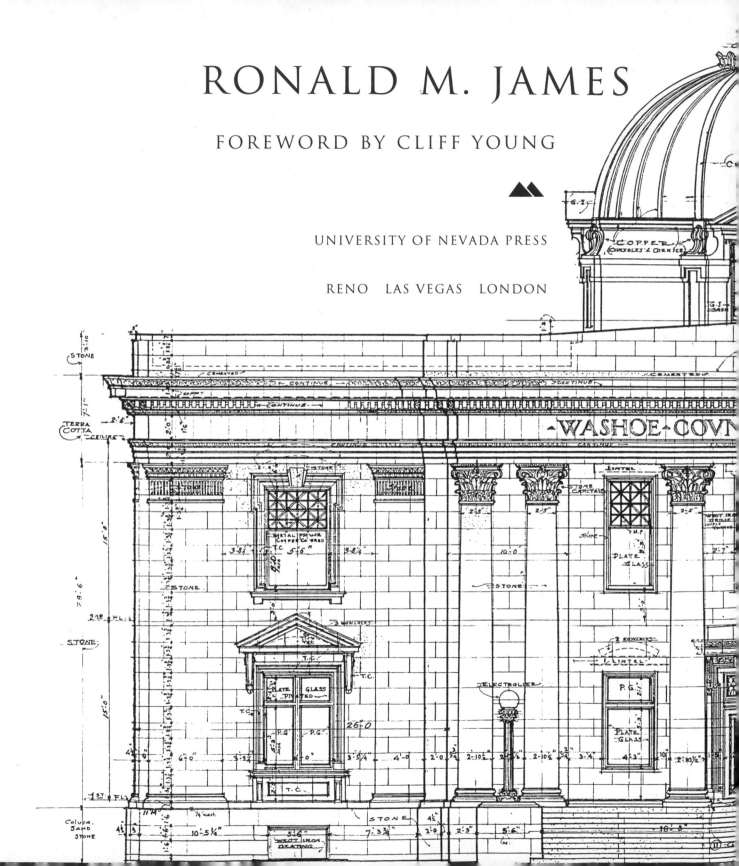

UNIVERSITY OF NEVADA PRESS

RENO   LAS VEGAS   LONDON

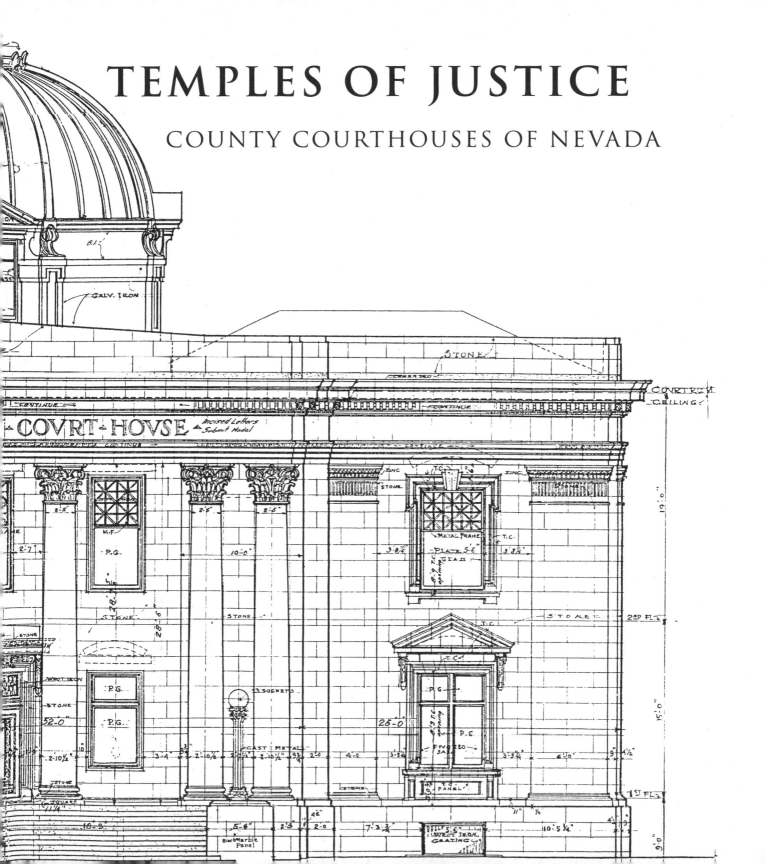

TEMPLES OF JUSTICE

COUNTY COURTHOUSES OF NEVADA

Wilbur S. Shepperson Series in
History and Humanities No. 35
Series Editor: Jerome E. Edwards

A list of books in the series follows the index.

Research for *Temples of Justice: County Courthouses
of Nevada* by Ronald M. James has been financed in
part with federal funds from the National Park Service,
a division of the U.S. Department of Interior, and
administered by the Nevada State Historic
Preservation Office.

Library of Congress Cataloging-in-Publication Data

James, Ronald M. (Ronald Michael), 1955–
    Temples of justice : county courthouses of Nevada /
by Ronald M. James.
        p. cm.—(Wilbur S. Shepperson series in history
and humanities)
    Includes bibliographical references and index.
    ISBN 0–87417–239-x (cloth : acid-free paper)
        1. Courthouses—Nevada—History. 2. Public
architecture—Nevada.
    I. Title. II. Series.
NA4472.N3J36 1994
725'.15'09793—dc20   93–37575
                                            CIP

University of Nevada Press, Reno, Nevada 89557 USA
Copyright © 1994 University of Nevada Press
Book and jacket design by Richard Hendel
Printed in the United States of America

9   8   7   6   5   4   3   2   1

To my family,

nuclear and extended,

literal and figurative—

they have always been

a source of strength

and joy.

CONTENTS

FOREWORD

James Madison penned in *The Federalist*, No. 51, over two centuries ago the following: "Justice is the end of government. It is the end of civil society. It ever has been and ever will be pursued. . . . "

The concern for justice—or perhaps fear of justice—was a matter of deep concern to Nevada's pioneers. Communities vied to be selected as the county seat where courthouses were built. The most impressive and expensive building in the county seat was usually the courthouse.

The story of the design, construction, and particularly the financing of these courthouses provides the basis for a fuller understanding of this exciting period in Nevada's past.

I congratulate Ronald M. James on an outstanding job in compiling this interesting facet of Nevada history and commend it to you.

Cliff Young, Justice
Supreme Court of Nevada

ACKNOWLEDGMENTS

Many individuals played crucial roles in the development of this manuscript, which is not unlike other projects of its size. *Temples of Justice* was initially conceived as part of Nevada's 200th anniversary celebration of the U.S. Constitution. The late Wilbur S. Shepperson inspired me when he pointed out that the Nevada State Historic Preservation Office (formerly the Division of Historic Preservation and Archeology of the State of Nevada Department of Conservation and Natural Resources) would be missing an opportunity if it did not contribute to this important commemoration. He was right. As a result, the National Park Service of the U.S. Department of the Interior, via the office, provided a grant to the Nevada Historical Society for an exhibit, poster, and publication based on this research. The Society's support and, in particular, that of Peter L. Bandurraga, Lee Mortenson, and Phillip I. Earl deserve a great deal of credit in furthering my work. Scott Klette of the Nevada State Museum and John Copoulos were helpful in preparing the illustrations for the manuscript. Similarly, the staff of the Nevada State Library and Archives, Mildred Syring of Getchell Library, University of Nevada, Reno (formerly of the Nevada State Library and Archives), and the staff from Special Collections, University of Nevada, Reno, patiently assisted me and searched for sources in a way that was above and beyond the call of duty. In the same way, Thomas R. Radko, Nicholas M. Cady, and Sara Vélez Mallea at the University of Nevada Press have always been helpful and courteous. I highly recommend all of their institutions.

In addition, there were a number of other individuals who helped me. They included various county commissioners and staff, district attorneys, and local librarians who conducted record searches and read portions of my manuscript. This is, in part, their book. I had hoped that it would inspire them to understand and to care for our significant courthouses. As it turned out, it has worked in the opposite way: The dedication and resourcefulness of local public employees all over the state inspired me. My particular thanks goes to Margaret Lowther, Storey County Recorder, for her assistance in acquiring the cover illustration for this book.

Several people spent many hours reviewing this manuscript and making comments on numerous drafts. Michael J. Brodhead, Russell R. Elliott, James W. Hulse, and William D. Rowley of the University of Nevada, Reno, and Candace Kant of the Community College of Southern Nevada, have all helped a great deal and they have my thanks. Jerome E. Edwards, history chair at the University of Nevada, Reno, was extremely helpful as editor of the Wilbur S. Shepperson History and Humanities Series of the University of Nevada Press. I also appreciated the encouragement of William A. Douglass, who is coordinator of the University's Basque Studies Program and former member of the University of Nevada Press Editorial Advisory Board. Robert E. Diamond, who has given me encouragement for decades, patiently read preliminary drafts and provided countless comments and suggestions. The late Edward Parsons also furnished information that he had accumulated after a distinguished career as a Nevada architect and his work on several courthouse rehabilitation projects.

Those who reviewed and commented on the text inevitably focused on its organization. Many felt that I should have arranged the material in chronological order rather than geographically. Texas served as model because there were two courthouse books, one with each approach. Texas, however, has 254 counties and Nevada does not. A county-by-county organization seemed to be the best treatment for Nevada and its thirty-four courthouses, but this approach aroused criticism. In response to the reviewers' suggestions, I wrote a chronological version of this text, and it failed largely because Nevada had too few examples to sustain the format. Those who reviewed the various versions were extremely helpful in assisting me to reach the conclusion that the county-by-county arrangement represented in this text was the only practical approach to the subject.

My thanks also goes to the people with whom I work and have worked: Roland Westergard, former director of the Department of Conservation and Natural Resources; his successor Peter Morros; Marcia Growdon and the members of the board of Museums and History; Scott Miller, the director of the Division of Museums and History; Joan Kerschner, the director of the Department of Museums, Library, and Arts; and Andria Daley and the Comstock Historic District Commission have all been generous with their support for this and similar projects. The same can be said of Margaret Pepin-Donat and her staff at the Western Regional Office of the National Park Service. Kathyrn M. Kuranda, former architectural historian with the office, originally planned to coauthor this publication. Although Kate left Nevada before fulfilling that goal, she was able to conclude some preliminary research that helped me considerably. More importantly, she taught me a great deal. This text bears her imprint. My thanks also goes to: Eve Tlachac, formerly of the office, Glen Clemmer of the Nevada Heritage Program, the staff at the Division of Museums and History, and William Fox, formerly of the Nevada State Council on the Arts. Special thanks go to Alice Baldrica, Gene Hattori, Susan Kastens, Michelle McFadden, and Bernadette Francke—my coworkers, colleagues, and friends—for unending support, encouragement, and their review of manuscript drafts. I would be surprised if a better team of dedicated hardworking souls exists anywhere.

Finally, my mother, my brother and his family, my father- and mother-in-law, Bill and his family, Ann and David, and Fran were a source of strength and revitalization when I needed to revise the manuscript. And of course, my wife Susan, a wonderful historian, writer, and person, has always been by my side with her critical mind, dogged reviews, and supportive friendship. This would not have been possible without her. It would also have been delayed had it not been for Reed, our energetic son. During the nine months of pregnancy, he took Susan's steam away, leaving countless quiet evenings while she slept and I conducted research, permitting me to complete what I could during that productive time, seven years ago. If she could have remained pregnant longer, I might have finished this manuscript sooner. Thanks, Reed, all the same.

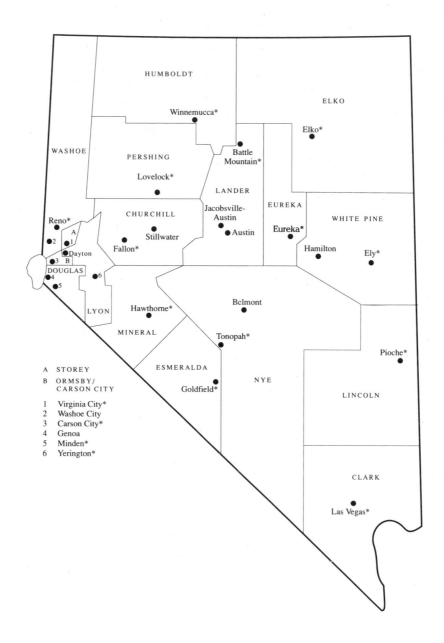

HUMBOLDT

ELKO

Winnemucca*

Elko*

WASHOE

PERSHING

Battle
Mountain*

Lovelock*

LANDER

EUREKA

WHITE PINE

CHURCHILL

Jacobsville-
Austin

Reno*

Stillwater

Austin

Eureka*

A

Hamilton

Ely*

2

1

Dayton

Fallon*

3   B

DOUGLAS

6

4

5

Belmont

LYON

Hawthorne*

MINERAL

Tonopah*

Pioche*

A   STOREY

B   ORMSBY/
    CARSON CITY

ESMERALDA

NYE

LINCOLN

1   Virginia City*
2   Washoe City
3   Carson City*
4   Genoa
5   Minden*
6   Yerington*

Goldfield*

CLARK

Las Vegas*

Locations of county courthouses in Nevada. Asterisks identify current county seats.

INTRODUCTION

Myron Angel, in his *History of Nevada* of 1881, asked: "A king without a kingdom, a general without an army, a county without a Court House— What are they?"[1] A courthouse, after all, can be a forceful statement of a community's wealth and its perception of self. It can stand as an architectural beacon from which people's pride and aspirations shine. Each Nevada county constructed at least one monumental courthouse in an attempt to express self-worth and lofty ideals.[2]

Most of the nation's 3,044 counties have probably been home to at least one impressive courthouse. Many have had two or three. Nevadans, however, have faced problems in planning public building projects. With nearly 87 percent of the state under federal management, Nevada's counties have not always commanded a sufficient tax base to support expensive construction efforts. This situation, common to much of the West, is all the more severe in Nevada.[3] The fact that leaders in each of the state's counties overcame financial limitations and pursued the erection of a monumental courthouse underscores the importance of stability and respectability that such buildings symbolize.

Because of their role as important local expressions of public architecture, courthouses provide an opportunity for us to understand the communities that designed and built them.[4] For example, the Humboldt County Courthouse stands as a testament to the stability and permanence of Winnemucca, while at the same time its southern sister in Lovelock speaks to the aspirations and optimism of a young Pershing County. Similarly, the courthouses in Tonopah, Goldfield, and Ely correspond to the explosive growth of turn-of-the-century mining towns. On the other hand, the grandeur of Storey County's facility results from the desire of Virginia City's leadership to perpetuate its nineteenth-century boom. These and all the other courthouse examples discussed in this work correspond to construction periods of local history. Similarly, state and national trends influenced the designs of Nevada's county courthouses, and the way the buildings collectively relate to their counterparts elsewhere reflects the state's character in a larger context. The position taken here is that physical structures illustrate local, state, and national history through design, scale, and building techniques. This is, in short, an architectural history of a portion of Nevada's buildings, an approach not previously undertaken in the state. The lack of such studies is unfortunate because buildings can serve, like any other primary document, as records containing valuable information about the past.[5]

Architectural analysis is shallow without historical context. Consequently, chapters two through eighteen include brief histories of each of Nevada's counties. The first chapter presents Nevada courthouses in the context of the region's past and the larger trends of public architecture. These buildings consequently provide an opportunity to comment on a part of Western and national history.

There is also an even larger context in which to understand the counties of Nevada. They are, after all, part of an old tradition of local government, passed on from medieval England to the New World. Indeed, the roots of the county draw more from an undocumented past than from legal records. Although the institution of local government began in England over a millennium ago, it was not codified there until the passage of the Local Government Act of 1888.[6] Before that time, the county government was akin to English common law and assumed to be the best way to manage the needs of the community. Of Anglo-Saxon origin, modified by Norman overlords, and codified only after the colonization of the New World, the county structure has served two continents as one of the most immediate and local systems of government and justice.

When English immigrants arrived in North America, they brought a tradition of local government with sheriffs, juries, judges, and the like. Without a system already in place, the colonists established their own in the New World, within the restraints of tradition and under the scrutiny of English government. In 1634 the Virginians partitioned their colony into eight shires or counties, each largely rural. A decade later, in 1643, the Massachusetts colony was divided into four counties, but this organization centered around communities. The settlement was the focus of Massachusetts local government, beginning a tradition of the New England town-hall meeting. The Massachusetts plan spread throughout New England, but the Virginia approach to land division was to dominate the other colonies and subsequently most of the country. Emphasizing the governing of the rural over the urban, the Virginia plan became the model for most Midwestern and Western states.

The Constitution of the United States of America, drafted in 1787 as an instrument of federal, national government, did not address the concerns of local governments, and so it had little effect on their development. Regional traditions thrived because the federal document left authority to the states. In fact, their constitutions tended to perpetuate and ratify local forms of county government.

By the mid-nineteenth century, the county became a ubiquitous feature of local governments throughout the nation.[7] The importance of the county, however, was not equally widespread. Where large urban communities incorporated, the city tended to overshadow the county government. In rural areas, however, the county remained the dominant form of local government. As author Calvin Trillin points out: "For a lot of Americans, 'County' still means country. It implies, at least, the absence of a big city."[8] Indeed, there is something *folksy* or *homey* about a county and its courthouse. It conjures images of children bicycling, cars slowing down at the town's only stoplight, and the courthouse functioning as the architectural centerpiece to an agricultural holiday fair in the town square. The image is, no doubt, inaccurate for many of the nation's county seats, but reality often reinforces stereotypes that, in themselves, become folklore. With roots in the time of the Anglo-Saxon yeoman who colonized Britain, the county is deeply ingrained in American culture. Even if this image is more ideal than real, the county and its government will probably continue to be an important part of America for a long time to come.[9]

As the tradition of county government spread to the West, it was adapted to regional conditions. The western Great Basin was first settled in the 1850s when entrepreneurs established stations to serve the pioneers as they crossed the continent. The arid land provided few opportunities for agricultural growth, and the region seemed to hold little promise for extensive development in the near future. Consequently, officials of the Utah Territory administered almost the entire Basin throughout the 1850s, even though its western reaches were far from Salt Lake City.

Mining changed the destiny of the region. The 1859 discovery of gold and silver on Mount Davidson began the "Rush to Washoe," a stampede to the western Great Basin. Territorial administration from Salt Lake City ceased to be practical. A new era began on March 2, 1861, with the creation of the Nevada Territory. Before the year ended, the territorial legislature began

These pre-1861 brass-press seals from Carson County (when it was still part of the Utah Territory) are among the earliest expressions of formal government in the western Great Basin. County officials used the seals to emboss important documents. These two photographs were reversed for easy reading. (James Gilmore)

creating counties, a process that continued into the twentieth century with Pershing County the last to be organized in 1919. County government allowed for closer administration of the growing population and ensured that enforcement of the law would be on hand. The burgeoning population, combined with President Lincoln's desire to have pro-Union senators endorsing his reconstruction legislation, inspired the elevation of Nevada to statehood on October 31, 1864.

The state born of mining, however, was also affected by its fluctuations. Nevada's economy throughout most of its history has been tied to an industry dependent on a nonrenewable resource, the price of which often corresponds to subtle shifts in national and international affairs. As a result, the state has often been subject to sudden collapses of some of its larger communities. The county seat of one period is an excellent candidate as a ghost town in another. In addition, much of the state has always been sparsely populated, with vast uninhabited por-

A QUESTION OF TITLE.

An early approach to the judicial process: "A fraction of the crowd . . . were engaged in a law suit relative to a question of title. The arguments used on both sides were empty whisky-bottles . . . or club law." From J. Ross Browne, A Peep at Washoe *(1860).*

tions managed by the federal government. These demographic and economic factors have influenced the state's courthouse history.

Nevada's county courthouses are important for many reasons, some of which are intangible. As symbols of the community, they convey the presence of law and authority and a sense of permanence and prosperity. At the same time, they serve as symbols of a past heritage. They are more than the official repositories of records. Locked within the bricks, plaster, concrete, and stone of the buildings are the decisions to build one year as opposed to the next, to build big rather than small, to build simply rather than with ornate details, to build in one place rather than another, and to save a physical structure rather than to demolish. In addition, courthouses

The laying of a cornerstone has always provided an opportunity for a community to celebrate. This ceremony for the Washoe County Courthouse dates to June 15, 1910. (Nevada Historical Society)

are often locally designed. County commissioners review and revise plans, and local artisans usually build the structures. County courthouses are, in fact, one of the most important, accessible symbols of law, government, and community. An appreciation of these important buildings can only serve, therefore, to better our understanding of ourselves and our past.

1 : JUSTICE IN BALANCE: DESIGN, SYMBOL & HISTORY

It is reasonable to see the construction of Nevada's county courthouses as a response to four different local, state, and national factors. First of all, popular opinion often affected the construction of courthouses. The state's low population permitted its citizens in the smaller centers of government to have more direct access to the decision-making process than was often the case in the nation's larger cities.

The state of the economy is the second factor that influenced Nevada courthouse architecture. Tied to the mineral industry through much of its history, Nevada benefited from times of boom and suffered from periods of economic depression. As the driest state in the nation's most arid region, Nevada never developed a substantial agricultural base nor attracted a large-scale manufacturing industry. Much of its past and, in particular, its courthouse history can be seen as a result of the effects of the peculiar circumstances of the mining West and its economic fluctuations. Economic cycles determined when courthouses could be built, and because of this it is possible to analyze this public architecture in four periods that coincide roughly with times of growth: from 1863 to 1865, 1869 to 1880, 1903 to 1922, and 1959 to 1973.

The ideal of *monumentality* in public architecture is a third factor that dominates all periods of courthouse construction in the state. Nevada's county courthouse architecture generally reflected the popular sentiment that public buildings should be grandiose, exhibit permanence and stability, and project an image of prosperity and respect for the institutions housed within. Monumentality implies large open spaces, ceilings higher than needed, doors taller than the standard 6½ or so feet, and oversized architectural features and details. The economy placed constraints on how this ideal would be manifested, but even in the more modest attempts at public architecture, the desire of Nevadans to project these ideals tended to shine through. The endeavor for monumentality in public architecture fitted into an international, timeless context, with examples from Stonehenge, the Egyptian temples, the U.S. Capitol, the British Parliament, and the Mayan and Aztec royal seats of power. Because of the region's austerity, Nevada's courthouses may be humble when compared to such exalted company, but monumentality was clearly the ideal sought and attained. The scale with which it is expressed in Nevada has consistently been diminutive, even in comparison with Western counterparts. Nevada's courthouses are clearly dwarfed by those of the more-populated and economically vibrant California, but they are also usually smaller than those of Utah and Idaho.[1] What is true of Nevada's county courthouses is also true for its other public buildings. Architectural historians Henry-Russell Hitchcock and William Seale point out that the Nevada State Capitol is one of the nation's smallest—smaller than many county courthouses in other states.[2] Nevertheless, even when built on a small scale, Nevada's county courthouses, like the state's capitol, have consistently achieved monumentality in their proportions.

Architectural style is the fourth factor that influenced Nevada's county courthouses. Unlike the ideal of monumentality, this factor was determined by the corresponding period of construction. Architectural fashions come and go, and the assortment of county courthouses built in the state illustrates the range of possibilities. Still, styles could be applied to public buildings only in certain ways; for example, borrowing from classical architecture for the designs of courthouses was a widespread practice. Because ancient Greece and Rome were thought to have inspired the nation's democracy, classical building design became pivotal at an early stage.[3]

During the colonial period of American history, increasing attention was given to architectural symbolism to enhance the process of justice, both outside and inside the building. The earliest court facilities tended to be stark rooms with little to designate function. Eventually, builders and magistrates gave more attention to the layout and furnishings of the courtroom. This trend progressed to the point where standard symbolism, as in the elevated platform with more elaborate molding that came to signify the magistrates' place, became commonplace in courthouse architecture.[4]

By the time the tradition of courtroom symbolism and design reached Nevada, American judicial architecture was formalized and sophisticated, and it has remained largely unaltered ever since. The bar, typically a balustrade or low wall, separates the public from the formal proceedings. Space is established for prosecutor and defendant, but there is no difference between the two in this balanced system where the accused is innocent until proven guilty. The jury is segregated from the proceedings by another wall or balustrade, apart and yet in the midst of the proceedings, with every opportunity for observation. Access to a rear door allows for removal of individuals without public interference. The witness box is closely associated with the judge's bench, itself a raised, ornamented, and focal point of the courtroom. The judge, like the jury, has a rear entrance into the courtroom separate from attorneys and the public alike. Variations

A gilded bracket decorates the second-floor ceiling of the 1880 Eureka County Courthouse and indicates the attention to detail typical of much of Nevada's courthouses. (Ronald M. James)

occur, but the symbolic language of elevation, balustrades, separate space, and classical details remains the same.

Apart from the four factors that in a general way influenced courthouse architecture in

Nevada, structural appearance also depended on the training of the designer and, at least during the nineteenth century, that education was often minimal and informal. This state of affairs within the architectural profession, common throughout the nation at the time, was exacerbated in Nevada. Portions of the Nevada wilderness were subjected to sudden development, and urban centers on such occasions quickly took root and attracted a full range of professionals, except for architects, who were often the last to arrive. It was not unusual for a county, which needed to build a facility, to have no architect to design one. While other frontiers faced similar dilemmas, Nevada's special position arose from the fact that the mining West, and the region in general, resulted in sudden urban growth.[5] Nevertheless, the mining industry included engineers and builders with the basic skills needed to construct a structurally sound courthouse.

The citizens of these instant cities, larger than many others in the West, frequently sought the conventional expressions of urbanity. Many of the nineteenth-century mining communities in Nevada acquired county-seat status within one to three years of their establishment. Thus, the leaders in Belmont (Nye County), Hamilton (White Pine County), and Unionville (Humboldt County) all began contemplating courthouse construction shortly after the boom periods that created the community. The wealth of the local economy and the attitudes of its entrepreneurs made monumental courthouse construction possible and desirable. Unfortunately, the courthouse was often completed after the boom began to fade, leaving the county with an investment in a community that otherwise might have been abandoned altogether. Nevada's role as an extreme example of the arid-mining West makes it an ideal case for understanding the region as a whole and, in particular, studying its public architecture as an outgrowth of regional conditions.

The designers of Nevada's nineteenth-century courthouses had varying access to education. Although the historical record on many of these individuals is sparse, it is clear that a few had considerable training in both academic and apprenticeship settings, while others applied themselves with no formal background in design. During this time period, there were eighteen courthouse architects in Nevada and almost no information on four. Two others were architects by training, five were professional builders, and seven represented a variety of other backgrounds. What the term *builder* meant is difficult to say. It was relatively common for architects to market themselves as carpenters or masons and for builders to have some training or experience in design. It seems likely that of the five who were builders, at least two had no design training. Four of the courthouse designers were involved in the mining industry, and they probably relied on their knowledge of structural engineering to plan substantial courthouses that would not collapse.[6]

Thus, much of what the architects designed for the counties of Nevada must be called *vernacular* architecture. This is a term applied to buildings that cannot be easily defined as representing standard architectural styles. In Nevada these buildings were generally freestanding with one to three stories. They frequently terminated in a gable or flat roof with projecting false fronts. Often, plain posts supported an open porch on the main façade. Ornamentation was generally minimal and restricted to the front entry, windows, and cornice. Nationally, vernacular design in public architecture normally occurred only in the first period of settlement, when civilization had but a tenuous hold on the area. Vernacular courthouse design in Nevada, however, lasted much longer, as an apparent expression of the mining West. As the state progressed from its initial settlement phase, mining boomtowns continued to play an important role. Many of the courthouses built in the more remote, new county seats represent collections of styles that warrant classification as vernacular, and this is as true of the turn-of-the-century examples as it was of those built in the 1860s.

The training of one of Nevada's most prolific and respected designers, Frederick J. DeLongchamps (also spelled as DeLongchant), serves to mark a transition in the architectural profession in Nevada. DeLongchamps, designer of seven courthouses in the state and two in California, received a mining-engineering degree in 1904 from the University of Nevada. Told he had a weak constitution, DeLongchamps changed careers and worked as a surveyor. The 1906 San Francisco earthquake created a demand for individuals associated with the building trades and attracted DeLongchamps and many others. He became an apprentice to a local architectural firm during the reconstruction of the city, and through this opportunity he acquired his only formal training in design. With his subsequent return to Nevada in 1907, he was in a position to market his skills and to dominate the field for the next fifty years. Although he never lost interest in the mining industry, the approximately five hundred designs that survive indicate the depth of his contribution to the state.[7] Since DeLongchamps's arrival on the Nevada scene, professionalism has dominated the field of architecture in the state and no county has built a courthouse that can be called vernacular.

The transition that occurred with DeLongchamps coincided with changes in the profession internationally. Architectural design as a field of study and training has been extremely rare throughout European and North American history. Buildings for the most part were erected by artisans who employed traditional methods of construction. By the nineteenth century metropolitan centers served as home to increasing numbers of professional architects who trained apprentices and eventually achieved licensing power over their peers. Since Nevada was late to participate in this process, it affected not only the development of the profession but also the design of its buildings.[8] The state that belatedly required training for its architects was also slow to employ the latest fashions in architecture. The 1870 Greek Revival Lander County Courthouse in Austin dates after the rest of the nation had all but abandoned the style for public buildings; similarly, the 1947 Mapes Hotel and Casino in Reno is one of the last major Art Deco structures ever constructed.

The modern techniques used in courthouses constructed after World War II required a better understanding of materials and structural foundations, and this knowledge was best obtained from a formal design training program. The building technology employed a skeleton

DeLongchamps designed the elaborate iron baluster for the 1909 Washoe County Courthouse.
(Ronald M. James)

of steel that could stand on its own. Glass and other finishing materials were then appended to the frame as an exterior veneer, as skin, not bone. Unlike older buildings, the walls no longer bear the weight of the structure. These buildings required a designer with training.

Regardless of the period of construction, many similar factors came into play to determine the appearance of a courthouse. The balance between individual tastes and talent, fashion, timeless symbolism, economics, and demography contributed to the county courthouses of Nevada. Whether to attract families or investors, these buildings helped communities create the desired self-image.[9] Even though certain common denominators tended to make courthouses similar, variations over time and space created differences.

Coming to terms with all the factors that contributed to the courthouse history of a state could assume nightmarish proportions. Texas, for example, has recently estimated that it has had about one thousand courthouses.[10] Since Nevada has only seventeen counties, a comprehensive examination of its county courthouses is a simpler proposition than those states with more local governments.[11]

The first era of courthouse building, from 1863 to 1865, coincides roughly with Nevada's territorial period. Because the immediate goal of the young counties was to provide shelter for local courts and government, most of the earliest courthouses were rented or purchased. During this period, four counties constructed new buildings, but they were unadorned and offered only the most essential of accommodations. With only limited means and resources, the counties met the urgent needs for housing judicial proceedings with these buildings. Clearly, such modest accommodations were part of a national trend in early settlements when securing shelter was the first and most crucial objective. Ornamentation and grandeur would come later. Still, within the context of this time period, these physical structures probably seemed impressive bastions of order.[12]

Perhaps the most influential architectural style of this period was Greek Revival, even if meagerly and belatedly applied in Nevada.[13] Popular nationally from 1820 to 1860, it was derived from the classic Greek temple and integrated details from Doric, Ionic, and Corinthian orders. In Nevada such structures were typically simple rectangular forms with gabled roofs facing the streets. Lintel cap windows were usually supported on both sides by square supports called posts. Exterior walls were as smooth as the construction material allowed. Exterior ornamentation was frequently lacking, although the cornice often included dentils (see figure in the glossary).[14]

Greek Revival architecture ran its course nationwide by 1860. Manifestations after that date are noteworthy as remnants of a style rejected for its overuse. But as was so often the case, Nevadans were late in getting the word. As mentioned earlier, Nevada boasts perhaps the nation's last Greek Revival courthouse, and this was part of a trend that continued for much of the state's history. Far from the East Coast, where artistic fashion first took hold, the West was the last to experience the ripple effect from pebbles dropped in the center of that cultural pond. And in Nevada, in the hinterland of the mining West, people were arguably even more out of touch. For much of its early history, those who colonized the West imported Eastern tastes and ideas. When the new Westerners applied this heritage in the region, they were not particularly innovative in their dealings with constitutions, law, or public architecture. The Western court-house, particularly of the nineteenth century, reflected conservatively applied styles that were popular in the East.

In spite of the late application of Greek Revival architecture, Nevadans followed the national trend in using the style for a wide variety of structures. Numerous houses in the state dating from the 1860s survived to illustrate its continued popularity.[15] Greek Revival architecture was particularly well suited for government buildings because of the visual reference to ancient Greece. Although the style eventually passed out of fashion, a national predilection to refer to classical motifs in courthouses has remained to the present.

The concern for style, monumentality, and availability of funds all influenced Nevada's second period of courthouse construction. Many of the state's counties built elegant courthouses from 1869 to 1883, exhibiting more formal architecture and in keeping with the time period when Nevadans were trying to stay in step with national trends. Finding shelter for local government was no longer a pressing issue. Nevada's counties demonstrated prosperity by erecting courthouses that projected a positive image of their communities. These courthouses served to contradict the critics who saw Nevada as "a dread sahara, unfit for habitation of man or beast."[16] Residents of the region faced considerable judgment of their homeland. Even the great promoter of westward migration, Horace Greeley, maintained that he was not referring to the Great Basin with his edict to "go West young man." He wrote:

> Who would stay in such a region one moment longer than he must? . . . I thought I had seen barrenness before . . . but I was green . . . Here, on the Humboldt, famine sits enthroned, and waves his scepter over a dominion expressly made for him . . . There can never be any considerable settlement here.[17]

To counter such predictions, courthouse architecture of this second period reflects the desire to show that civilization and stability had taken hold in Nevada.

Although there are some late expressions of Greek Revival architecture during this period, the most commonly employed style was Italianate, popular nationally from 1860 to 1895. The style's influence extended to most nineteenth-century and turn-of-the-century Nevada buildings including its courthouses. The style is characterized by tall, symmetrical designs accented by arched door and window openings. Frequently, the distinguishing feature of the style is an ornate, bracketed cornice banding the eaves of the structure (see figure in the glossary). Italianate architecture includes motifs from ancient Greece. Architects frequently employed stylized pilasters, half columns adhered to the façade to give public buildings a classical appearance.[18] The Eureka and Storey County Courthouses are two outstanding surviving examples of this style.

Together with other examples of Italianate architecture, these buildings mark a time when Nevada came close to being in step with national tastes. This period's courthouses, then, did more than assert that civilization had arrived on the mining frontier; they also professed that Nevada participated in sophisticated cultural trends. Nevertheless, there are other courthouses in the state that exhibit the influence of Italianate with only a few motifs. These buildings were hybrids of Italianate and Greek Revival architecture and demonstrated that the vernacular continued as a force.

There were no major courthouses erected in Nevada during the two decades of mining depression and economic stagnation after 1883. With the turn of the century, prosperity returned and people swarmed to new mining towns. Shifts in population and a flood of wealth in the economy prompted county-seat changes and convinced Nevadans that they needed new courthouses worthy of their promising future. Changes in county seats were certainly nothing new; the first in Nevada occurred in 1863 when the Lander County government offices were moved from Jacobsville to Austin. Although there appears to have been little or no controversy over this change, some of the most hotly debated political contests in the state, as with the nation in general, have been over this kind of issue. Capturing a county seat was an important move for a community because local government could be a lucrative industry. Established county-seat officials often fought vigorously to retain hold of the government, but contenders were often equally determined. Fluctuations in the mining industry, however, caused many county seats to dwindle to the point where it was not realistic to resist attempts to move the center of government.[19]

The turn-of-the-century Nevada mining boom inspired a more recent cycle of such relocations. Whether in new or old seats of government, twelve growing Nevada counties constructed courthouses between 1903 and 1922. Most of the courthouses built after 1900 were not frantic responses to the need of shelter, nor were they attempts to demonstrate that civilization had come to the Great Basin. These structures were grand and massive, and they declared that civilization had advanced and was securely in place. Beyond that common attribute, the courthouses built between 1903 and 1909 seem to defy classification as a single group. For example, the Churchill County Courthouse, with its orderly, conventional use of Neo-Classical architecture, stands apart from the others—none of which exhibits any single architectural style. The Churchill County Courthouse, however, was yet another kind in the minority: It served an agricultural community at a time when mining was capturing the newspaper headlines.

The early twentieth-century mining boom paralleled the first settlement period of Nevada in many ways. Both occurred at a time when the government and the courts could not keep pace with the creation of new communities, and both were followed by the construction of courthouses that involved an eclectic approach to architecture. Built within six years of one another, the three turn-of-the-century mining-boomtown courthouses in Tonopah, Goldfield, and Ely exhibited elements of at least four different architectural styles—each lacking a clear expression of any one. The use of several styles, in vernacular adaptations, was part of a larger trend in the West for turn-of-the-century courthouses.[20]

Some of the design choices of this period were influenced by Mission Revival architecture. Popular from about 1880 to 1935, this approach to design first appeared in California before the turn of the century as a celebration of the Southwest's past and as a reaction to Eastern styles that dominated the architecture of the period. Mission Revival buildings typically have tiled roofs, rounded arches, and plastered or smooth finishes. Occasionally, the style employs parapets, often with sweeping lines. Mission Revival was unique to the West, and its diffusion from California represents a true success in the region's effort to be culturally distinct from the East.[21] The eclectic adaptation of Mission Revival motifs, apparent in the vernacular courthouses of Nevada's hinterland, reflects a region striking out on its own and the artistic immaturity of its remote outposts. Once again, civilization had only a tenuous grasp on the fledgling mining towns of Nevada.

The eight courthouses built in Nevada between 1911 and 1922 stand in marked contrast to

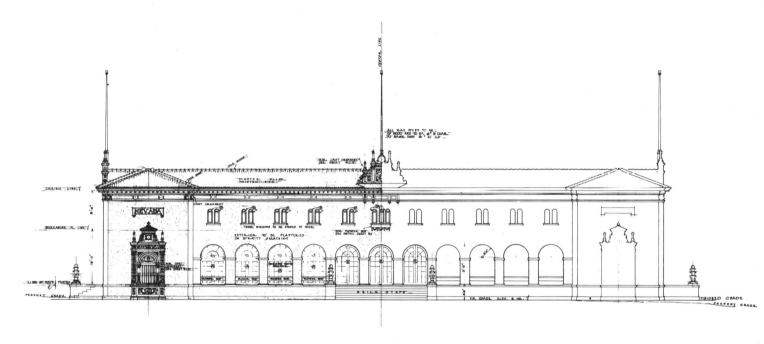

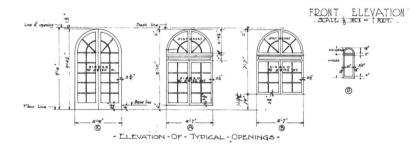

DeLongchamps's 1914 Mission Revival design for the Nevada State Building for the Panama-California Exposition in San Diego. (The DeLongchamps Collection, Getchell Library, University of Nevada, Reno)

those that preceded them. County officials constructed these buildings in more stable communities that tended to undertake public building more carefully. County seats with long-standing economic and social foundations built these new courthouses, which consequently did not rely on vernacular, local designs. Instead, these temples of justice, some of the most monumental in Nevada, were in step with national tastes and conventions. They stand out in their communities and leave no doubt about the significance of their undertaking. More importantly, however, this period was dominated by DeLongchamps, who designed seven Nevada courthouses. Of the courthouses built between 1911 and 1922, only that of Elko represents the work of someone else.

The Neo-Classical style of architecture, popular nationwide from about 1900 to 1930, prevailed in the second decade of twentieth-century courthouse construction. These buildings were monumental with restrained ornamentation and symmetrical geometric plans. Frequently constructed by masons, the style of these structures reveals classical Greek and Roman architectural themes and favor post-and-lintel openings and sculptured cornices. Even though Neo-Classical buildings tend to be larger in scale and more ornate than those of Greek Revival, they clearly represent a return to the same source of inspiration. This style provided the nation with some of its most monumental classical façades.[22] Nevada, particularly with the work of DeLongchamps, stepped quickly into fashion.

In his exploration of Neo-Classicism, DeLongchamps worked with a regional variation that can be regarded as a precursor of Spanish Colonial Revival architecture. This style evolved from Mission Revival architecture after the turn of the century. Although lacking a clear distinction from its predecessor, Spanish Colonial Revival buildings frequently include post-and-lintel openings and columns. The style did not receive a formal debut until 1915, but it was anticipated by the work of a few architects who experimented with the forms before that date.[23] DeLongchamps's Clark County Courthouse in Las Vegas, designed in 1913, was revolutionary for its early work with the motifs. Besides being the only monumental Spanish Colonial Revival structure built in the state, the courthouse clearly demonstrated that Nevada could be on the cutting edge. At least in its urban centers, Nevada was rising above its role as a cultural backwater.

Elaborate forms of early twentieth-century styles are sometimes referred to as Beaux-Arts Classicism architecture, taking its name from the École des Beaux-Arts, the Parisian school of design. This school exerted a major influence upon American architecture in the late nineteenth century. Beaux-Arts buildings are usually distinguished by their monumental scale and elaborate classical ornamentation. The symmetrical designs frequently incorporate raised basements, projecting wings, detailed cornices, and grand entries. The structures are generally built in masonry and often include central domes. The Beaux-Arts style was particularly well suited to public and important commercial buildings. Classification of a structure as Neo-Classical, Spanish Colonial Revival, or anything else other than Beaux-Arts Classicism is often a matter of degree and opinion; the former styles have simpler composition and ornamentation than classical architectural styles. The existing courthouses in Reno and Elko, with their massive wings, heavy columns, and reliefs, come the closest of any structure in Nevada to Beaux-Arts architecture. The design approach was well suited for massive, monumental public buildings and it provides the nation with some of its more impressive façades. In Nevada, however, economic constraints often prohibited building on such a scale. That only two of the many courthouses of the period can even aspire to the title of Beaux-Arts architecture speaks, once again, to the financial limitations that Nevada counties faced.

The few county courthouses built in the state after 1922 depart from classical architectural styles. County officials approved modern designs for these newer courthouses, but factors other than style set these structures apart from their predecessors. These buildings tend not to serve as symbols of prosperity and law and order, nor do they serve as the community's focal point. The architectural style is also correspondingly different and simplified because of the concern for practicality in today's world.

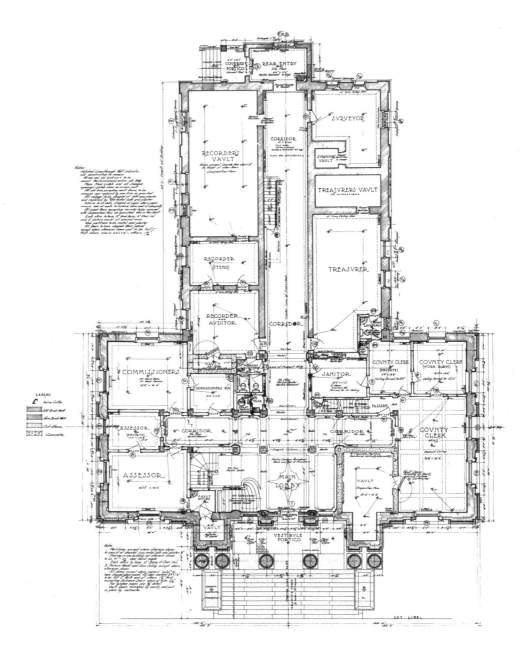

A 1909 floor plan for Washoe County Courthouse, designed by DeLongchamps, features advancing and receding planes, especially on the front elevation, and is indicative of Beaux-Arts massing. (The De-Longchamps Collection, Getchell Library, University of Nevada, Reno)

Earlier courthouses made use of formal, monumental entries, halls, and courtrooms to emphasize the ceremonial nature of government. These older structures contrast with the more recent utilitarian courthouses. With classical details stylized or abandoned after the 1920s, much of what was archetypal courthouse architecture disappeared. As suggested by the *Courthouse Conservation Handbook*: "The dominant concept has been that county offices have the same requirements as commercial offices."[24] This, combined with a growing need for work space, has inspired the construction of buildings distinct from their predecessors but not from their modern commercial counterparts. These courthouses were usually built in the International style with flat roofs, smooth wall surfaces, skeleton construction of steel or concrete, and a lack of ornamentation (see the photograph of the 1958 Clark County Courthouse in chapter 4). The International style, a descendant of the Bauhaus style that originated in Germany as early as 1919, was popularized in America in 1932 during the first exposition of architecture at the Museum of Modern Art in New York. Popular nationwide from about 1930 to 1950, the International style continues to influence some architecture. The cost effectiveness of its simple construction techniques contributed to the national popularity of International architecture and made it particularly well suited for Nevada.

The courthouses of Nevada, in the first three eras of construction, are part of a continuous evolution of one style to the next, with a consistent reliance on classical motifs. Most of these structures project a courthouse image. The fourth and most recent phase of construction, however, deviates from this pattern. These courthouses lack majestic entrances and interior spaces, and ornamentation is rare or absent. Instead, their form is like other buildings of their time from which they are indistinguishable. As architectural historian Albert Larson points out, these courthouses "depend on discreet signs with block lettering to identify their purpose."[25]

The most recent period of Nevada courthouse construction is also unlike the previous ones in its random pattern of development. These modern projects do not represent a burst of activity in response to a statewide economic boom. Instead, the courthouses respond to local needs and date from times of local prosperity. In addition, there is a tendency to refer to the newer facilities as law enforcement centers, which only house the sheriff, courts, and jail. The county commissioners and other county officials reside in other buildings or remain in the older courthouse.

The most recent era of courthouse construction has also involved the rehabilitation of existing structures. Many county officials, lacking the funds or unwilling to construct new buildings, have modernized the older courthouses. Nye County, for example, cloaked its distinctive Romanesque entrance with a steel and glass porch; White Pine County replaced the doors and windows of its courthouse to make it more energy efficient; and other counties have made similar alterations. These rehabilitation programs, together with the construction of additions and annexes, have been local attempts to update public buildings without the expense of new construction. Perhaps the desire to keep an old structure because of community pride also played a part in these decisions. The ultimate expression of this trend occurred in 1979 when Lander County officials, having moved from Austin, occupied a former school in Battle Mountain. The remodeled 1916 structure had the same ceremonial trappings as other Neo-Classical courthouses in Nevada. With sensitive rehabilitation, county officials avoided the cost of new construction and obtained a grand courthouse in the historical tradition of the state.

Even though architectural styles varied throughout the state, the concern for economizing was prevalent in all courthouse construction periods. County officials consistently strived for a substantial courthouse while also conserving funds. Although this is probably a national preoccupation, the large percentage of public lands and the limited tax base of Nevada has reinforced the predilection for thriftiness.[26] Predictably, this has often resulted in the design of modest buildings, on a small scale, to serve limited populations and has reflected the state's regional and national role as an arid outback. Still, Nevada's courthouses are a testament to the ability of a few people to do a great deal with very little. Collectively, the courthouses stand out as monuments to the perseverance of its citizens and their determination in the face of a hostile environment.

During the past 130 years, Nevadans have erected more than thirty courthouses in their seventeen counties. Although almost one-third of them are now gone, each that remains is an important symbol of state and local history. In addition, they serve as clear statements of Nevada's place in the region and nation. Nevada architects, with their initial vernacular attempts to mimic national trends, staggered behind the avant-garde. Indeed, this remained true for each new mining frontier throughout its hinterland for the first fifty years of the state's history. After this long period of gestation, Nevada reached a point where its courthouses were in step with national trends.

The architects, in employing styles that value symmetry, succeeded in designing courthouses that function as metaphors for the ideal of the judicial process and of the local government. As with the scales of Lady Justice herself, these monuments generally exhibit balance and order and serve as sturdy focal points that instill confidence and pride in the community.

2 : CARSON CITY & ORMSBY COUNTY

It is difficult to perceive a single identity for Carson City because it serves as the seat of local government and the state capital. Too often the state's history and architecture overshadows that of the city of Carson. Nevertheless, the Neo-Classical Ormsby County Courthouse in Carson City stands in harmony with the surrounding state buildings. The courthouse is adjacent to the impressive former State Supreme Court and Library Building and is dwarfed by the capitol across the street, both excellent architectural examples contributing to Carson City's identity problem. In addition, two doors down is the State Heroes Memorial Building, a twin of the county facility, which makes the courthouse all the more unremarkable.

In 1858 Abraham Curry founded Carson City in the vicinity of Eagle Station, a trading post decorated with the remains of its namesake. Curry named his town site after Christopher "Kit" Carson (1809–1868), who explored the western Great Basin with John C. Frémont in the winter of 1843–1844.[1] Although Curry planned his community while it was still part of the Utah

Territory, he ambitiously set aside a portion of the town site for the erection of a state capitol. It was not uncommon for town fathers to set aside land for a courthouse in hopes of attracting the seat of county government, but Curry's optimism was unrestrained. Still, his foresight was well grounded. The discovery of the nearby Comstock Lode in 1859 resulted in explosive growth in the area. Carson City was well situated to serve as a mercantile center for the new mining district. While still part of the Utah Territory, the community subsequently grew larger than Genoa, its southern neighbor, and became the new government seat of Carson County. When Nevada territorial governor James Warren Nye arrived with other appointed officials in 1861, to assume his position in Carson City, Curry's vision for his community was nearing reality.[2]

The Nevada territorial legislature created Ormsby County on November 25, 1861, and named it after Major William M. Ormsby, who died in 1860 while leading the Carson City Rangers during the Pyramid Lake Indian War. Because its government seat was also a territorial (and then state) capital, Ormsby County did not need to erect a new courthouse to gain credibility. Indeed, in 1862 the commissioners purchased the Great Basin Hotel from Abraham Curry for $42,500.[3] Angel pointed out in 1881 that it was "not conspicuous as a public building nor particularly ornamental."[4] The *Carson Daily Appeal* sarcastically went further:

> A stranger crossing the plaza to the northwest cannot fail to be struck with the architectural beauty and complete design of our County Court House, nor fail to be impressed with the fact that it is unique in its ungainly, unattractive, elongated proportions, not to mention the awning and porch.[5]

In spite of these opinions, Ormsby County officials retained the structure for almost sixty years, far longer for a purchased facility than in any other Nevada county.

When Curry platted the Carson City town site, he planned major arteries, from east and west, pointing toward the capitol site. The capitol was to face the north-south main street, ensuring its effect as a monumental presence and as the center of the community. In spite of Curry's vision, his capitol site lay dormant for several years after Nevada's territorial status was changed to statehood. Oddly, Curry did not set aside a courthouse site of equal dignity. Almost by chance, the Ormsby County Courthouse came to reside on the main street, nearly opposite the capitol grounds. Clearly, the emphasis of Curry's town plat was for the future capitol, and ever since Carson City has had difficulty establishing an identity distinct from that of the state government. In fact, Ormsby County Courthouse history can only be understood in the context of state and federal government architecture.

The Great Basin Hotel in Carson City served as the Ormsby County Courthouse for several decades until its demolition in 1920. (Nevada Historical Society)

The capitol in Carson City has a strong Italianate design and dominates the public architecture of the community. This early photograph shows it shortly after construction in 1871. (Nevada Historical Society)

The Nevada State Capitol, the U.S. Mint, and the U.S. Post Office and Courthouse buildings were all completed between 1869 and 1891, in a century that saw no Ormsby County courthouse construction. Unchallenged by any competing community that was striving for county-seat status and supplied with impressive architectural structures without county expense, Carson City failed to participate in both nineteenth-century periods of Nevada courthouse construction from 1863 to 1865 and from 1869 to 1880. Indeed, it was twenty years into the next century before Carson City's county government sought to attain a courthouse architectural identity, and even this was soon overshadowed by the State Supreme Court and Library Building.

In 1920 Ormsby County commissioners received design plans for their new courthouse from DeLongchamps, who was then serving as Nevada State Architect. He copied his plans for the State Heroes Memorial Building, named in honor of World War I veterans, and used them to construct both buildings on the same block. In fact, the plans for the courthouse reveal the title "Ormsby County Court House" printed over "Heroes Memorial." In addition DeLongchamps's title appears only as "Architect," with the name "State Architect," which was written on the plans for the memorial building, visible only as a shadow because it had been erased.[6] These adjustments permitted DeLongchamps, as state architect, to also furnish the plans to local government officials for their use. The plans allowed the county building to be in architectural balance with the state Capitol Complex.

In February 1920 the Ormsby County commission accepted the bid of C. G. Sellman, of Reno, to build the courthouse. Sellman's low bid of $65,735 was well above the $47,800 limit of available funds, and so the commissioners eliminated some features such as "lighting and heating, plumbing, interior finishings and cornice work" with the idea that they could go before the 1921 legislature to obtain additional bonds to finish the project.[7] The commission began demolition of its sixty-year-old hotel-turned courthouse, a local landmark in its own right. Sellman initially proceeded with caution so that he could acquire timber and stone for the new project, but it soon became apparent that the demolition called for more drastic measures.[8] The massive stone structure did not destruct easily as the local *Appeal* observed: "It was a well put together edifice and the use of large quantities of powder has been necessary in breaking down the walls."[9]

The contractor unceremoniously laid the cornerstone in place during an August afternoon in 1920. Only a few days before the event, the *Appeal* called for donations of material to be placed inside, but it appears that there were no responses. Lacking the attention normally afforded such an occasion, the newspaper reported that "no ceremony will be held [when] the Contractor . . . drops the stone into place."[10] Perhaps a community with a state capitol and a courthouse, the

· FRONT · ELEVATION ·

The 1920 Neo-Classical Ormsby County Courthouse by DeLongchamps. (The DeLongchamps Collection, Getchell Library, University of Nevada, Reno)

mere copy of a secondary state office building, felt little need to celebrate its public architecture. As with the first hotel-turned courthouse, this new facility, which in any other county seat would have served as an important architectural beacon, could not compete with other structures.

With the necessary funds secured to complete the project, county officials occupied the new courthouse on March 16, 1922, after more than two years of construction. Although DeLongchamps probably designed it before he worked on the Pershing County Courthouse, this Carson City building was his last county courthouse opened in Nevada. The two-story symmetrical Neo-Classical structure has a hipped roof made of standing seam tin. The entrance consists of a porch supported by a row of columns of massive Tuscan-order supports. Above is a classical pediment, a triangular gable dominating the roof line of the building. State prisoners quarried its large limestone blocks from the Carson City prison site as they had for the capitol and its additions, for the State Heroes Memorial Building, and for many other local public buildings.

Although the Ormsby County Courthouse was a replica of the State Heroes Memorial Building, its interior differed from the state structure. The courthouse had four jail cells on the second story, next to the sheriff's office. The courtroom on the north side of the second story had carpeting on its opening day and, according to the local newspaper, it boasted: "first-class electrical fixtures."[11] The first floor provided offices for various officials and for the justice of the peace; the recorder occupied half of the basement.

State officials began investigating the possibility of erecting a new supreme court building in the mid-1930s. For over sixty years the highest judicial body in the state met in the state capitol. A growing staff and library created the need for a separate building. A design by DeLongchamps called for a refined execution of Art Deco architecture, including an exterior graced by stylized sunbursts and other details. DeLongchamps designated black marble and aluminum to decorate the interior. His plans also included a sixteen-point star of cathedral glass to serve as the ceiling of the second-story courtroom. In 1937 the Supreme Court moved into the new building, which remains the state's finest Art Deco courthouse.[12]

Situated between the Ormsby County Courthouse and the State Heroes Memorial Building, the new state court structure challenged the architectural uniformity of the area. In addition, the new building obstructed the impressive view of the capitol on King Street. The completion of the State Supreme Court and Library Building, only a few years after the construction of its adjacent county building, provided an epilogue to local courthouse architectural history: More than ever, the Ormsby County Courthouse became part of and subservient to the architecture of the state complex.

DeLongchamps's Ormsby County Courthouse continues to serve Carson City. This photograph probably dates to the time of the building's completion in 1922. (Nevada Historical Society)

After the 1969 consolidation of Ormsby County and Carson City into an independent municipality, the courthouse became a city facility. In the 1990s the state began considering the purchase of the building to expand the Capitol Complex. This provides yet another example of the relationship between the state and local government as expressed in Carson City architecture. Already, much of the Carson City government and jail occupied facilities scattered throughout the community. The loss of the old Ormsby County Courthouse to the state will amplify the lack of an architectural focal point already felt in Carson City.

3 : CHURCHILL COUNTY

For the first forty years of its existence, the seat of Churchill County government moved from one town to another, and officials occupied several courthouses. It was not until after the turn of the century that they constructed a courthouse that could serve as an architectural focal point for the county and its government in Fallon. As the only monumental courthouse in Nevada built of wood, the structure survives today as a ceremonial entrance to the Churchill County complex. The courthouse history of the county before construction of this building, however, reflects aimlessness and economic poverty.

On November 25, 1861, the government of the Nevada Territory established Churchill County in the central part of the state and named it after the Fort Churchill military post—itself honoring Brigadier General Sylvester Churchill. Lyon County commissioners administered the area, which is now Churchill County, until February 19, 1864. Before Churchill County became a separate entity, settlers along the Carson River petitioned to have the area surrounding the military post permanently annexed to Lyon County. As a result, Fort Churchill is not in the county for which it was named. This early history serves to illustrate Churchill County's status among its peers: The last of the originally created 1861 counties to be organized, it was one of the poorest and it easily fell victim to the ambitions of its neighbors.

La Plata, a mining camp in the southern foothills of the Silver Hill Range, was the county's first seat. Its courthouse was a dwelling acquired on October 15, 1864, for $700 from Anton Kaufman. By 1867 La Plata's mining boom declined and support for moving the county seat gained momentum. In a special election held on October 22, 1867, the electorate cast thirty-three

The 1885 wooden courthouse at Stillwater no longer exists. It served Churchill County until after the turn of the century, when the government seat moved to Fallon. (Nevada Historical Society)

votes for relocating the county government to Stillwater; only seventeen voted for a move to Big Adobe, a small way station to the west.

When the Churchill County seat moved to Stillwater in December 1868, officials dismantled the house-turned-courthouse in La Plata and reassembled it in the new location. Eventually finding the one-room wooden structure unsuitable, they finished construction on a more permanent two-story courthouse in 1870. Although little is known about the building, it appears to have had a standard configuration, with the courtroom on the second floor above the jail and county offices.[1] Marcia de Braga in *Dig No Graves* maintains that it was a 16 x 24-foot structure with the jail below in an unfinished hole.[2] Unfortunately, the county failed to secure clear title to the land, and in 1883 the property owner, upon discovering the problem, claimed the courthouse as his own.

After being evicted, the Churchill County commissioners were faced again with the need to secure accommodations. Local mines were not productive at the time, however, and without their revenues an elaborate building program was out of the question. The commission rented a house for $5 a month until a new wooden courthouse could be completed in 1885 for $3,900.[3] The modest two-story structure with a rock foundation was spanned by a two-story deck porch. In addition, it had a false-front façade much like the majority of Western commercial buildings of the period.

Under the national Newlands Reclamation Act of 1902, the ambitious movement for the irrigation and cultivation of thousands of acres of desert caused a shift in population in Churchill County. On March 5, 1903, the county seat moved from Stillwater to Fallon, the center of new agricultural growth. The vibrant community took on an appearance unlike that of a mining boomtown. Town leaders organized Fallon on a well-platted plan distinct from the spontaneous growth of a mining camp. Although sudden in its inception and early development, Fallon rapidly assumed the appearance of a stable agricultural community. The county commissioners

The Churchill County Courthouse in Fallon, with its two-story portico and classical features, is now the only wooden courthouse in Nevada. (Photo ca. 1904; Nevada Historical Society)

quickly planned the construction of a new courthouse. For $100 Reno architect Ben Leon designed a two-story Neo-Classical frame building. W. B. Wyrick, a Fallon builder, won the construction contract for $7,300. Warren and Addie Williams and John Oats donated the land for the facility. While planning for its new courthouse, the county commissioners sold its old Stillwater building to Alber Weishaupt, who dismantled it for materials. The county accepted the new structure in February 1904.

The principal elevation of the Fallon courthouse is spanned by a large two-story pedimented portico (the front porch) supported by paired Ionic columns. A masonry foundation supports the building that rises to a hipped roof and is sheathed in asphalt shingles. A hipped roof cupola incorporating stylized fan lights stands above the entry portico. A simple board cornice marks a slightly extended eaves line. Narrow weatherboard sheaths the three-bay courthouse with simple boards defining the corners. As is the case with the majority of Nevada's courthouses, the building has a central hall flanked by rows of offices, and the courtroom is located on

DeLongchamps's 1948 proposal for the Churchill County Courthouse in Fallon is dominated by the International style, although an influence from the Moderne style is evident in the sleek lines and the mass above the door. (The DeLongchamps Collection, Getchell Library, University of Nevada, Reno)

the structure's upper floor. Churchill County officials intended its monumental building to be permanent and impressive, in contrast with all others who built wooden courthouses in the state. This building was not a temporary measure.[4]

As early as the 1940s, Churchill County officials felt a need for more room and employed DeLongchamps to propose options for a new courthouse.[5] The county, however, did not pursue his plans. In the 1970s the county began work on a sizeable two-story law enforcement facility designed by Raymond Hellman of Reno and built by the Argus Construction Company. Dedicated in 1973 this building now houses the county courtroom and law-enforcement services. The structure stands behind the Neo-Classical turn-of-the-century courthouse that functions as the ceremonial entrance to the complex and continues to be used by the county for offices. Fallon's agriculturally based foundation makes it unusual in the state. The courthouse is wooden and serves as a symbol of the unique history of the county.

4 : CLARK COUNTY

Nevada's southernmost county has had three courthouses in one seat of government. Clark County was not organized until 1909, making its rapid succession of courthouses a testimony to its phenomenal growth. Furthermore, its three public buildings demonstrated a full range of scale, cost, and design and expressed in architecture the profound changes that the community witnessed since it began as a railroad town in 1905.

Clark County, in many ways a child of the railroad industry, has its roots in the turn-of-the-century mining boom of southern and central Nevada. The wealth of those areas spilled over to many nonmining communities in Nevada. The Las Vegas railroad connection in southern Lincoln County served as a distribution point for the new central-Nevada mining districts. The residents of the early, diminutive Las Vegas were part of the nation's largest county, and they faced a formidable trip when they wanted to conduct business in Pioche—the county seat to the far north. Soon after 1905, when Las Vegas became a major point on the San Pedro, Los Angeles & Salt Lake Railroad, southern Nevada residents began to call for the creation of a new county.

At the same time, the Lincoln County commissioners were considering the replacement of the courthouse in Pioche. The debt for the thirty-year-old facility was still not settled, and, in fact, interest on the loan had swelled far beyond its original cost, causing the structure to earn the nickname "The Million Dollar Courthouse." When the citizens of the southern, distant part of Lincoln County heard that the commissioners might replace their public facility before settling the debt, the call for county division began in earnest. Eventually, the residents of Las Vegas and its neighbors took their case to the Nevada State Legislature, which divided Lincoln County and its courthouse debt. As a result, on July 1, 1909, Clark County acquired a deficit of almost a half million dollars, a burden unmatched in Nevada history.[1]

The original 1905 plan for Las Vegas set aside a block of land for a courthouse square. Optimistic civic leaders raised $1,800 for the construction of the courthouse and completed the project before organizing the county. The unadorned, square, and concrete building included a Mission Revival parapet reminiscent of that used in the contemporaneous Esmeralda County Courthouse in Goldfield. The simple courthouse symbolized a time when Las Vegas looked to Goldfield as the region's population and cultural center. The Clark County commission held its first meeting on July 3, 1909, in its tiny facility, which served as a courthouse for only a few years.[2]

In 1914 the county commissioners erected a larger structure with a distinguished design by DeLongchamps. This, his third courthouse, departed from his previous conservative adaptations of Neo-Classical motifs. For Nevada's only county seat with a Spanish name, he appropriately

designed a courthouse that anticipated Spanish Colonial Revival architecture. As suggested by the *Las Vegas Age* in 1913:

> The design is founded on the Spanish renaissance which is especially appropriate to this county both by reason of its historical associations, the Vegas Valley having been first explored by the Spaniards, as well as on account of the semi-tropical character of its climate.[3]

With this plan, the architect demonstrated his flexibility and his genius for drawing upon local tastes.[4] He did not force a traditional Neo-Classical design into the southern railroad town. Instead, DeLongchamps experimented with motifs inspired by the Hispanic heritage of the Southwest, and in so doing he anticipated a style that architectural historians regard as not having a formal debut for two more years. At the same time, DeLongchamps included some Neo-

Classical elements into the courthouse design, which unified it with his previous work. In fact, the Clark County Courthouse represented a synthesis that created a symbol of stability, grace, and authority. At the same time, it pioneered a new regional architecture.

His plans, drafted in 1913, called for a 60 x 100-foot two-story masonry building with a red tile roof. The design provided for some windows to have round arches and others to be rectangular. Low-relief carvings surrounded the second-story end-bay windows, which are separated by

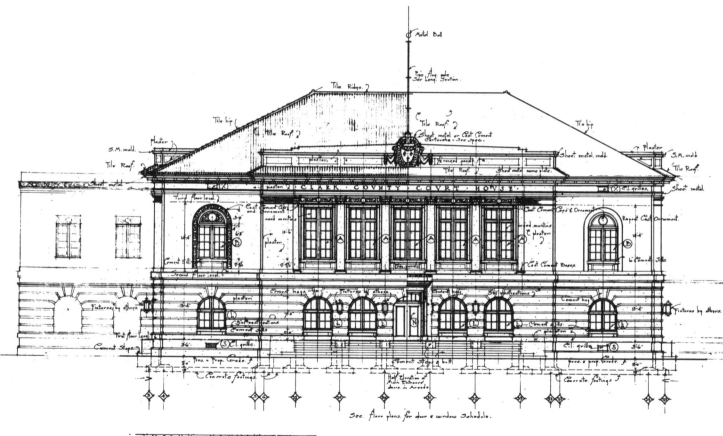

DeLongchamps's 1914 Spanish Colonial Revival design for the Clark County Courthouse in Las Vegas. (The DeLongchamps Collection, Getchell Library, University of Nevada, Reno)

Corinthian columns. An entablature was to include a projecting, bracketed cornice, a decorated frieze, and a stepped parapet with a central cartouche.

The design plan entailed 45-foot-long concrete steps, rising dramatically to the building's front entrance arcade, which was 12 x 42 feet long and graced with Mission Revival arches. It made for a distinguished presentation. The entrance opened to four marble steps leading to the main foyer. The first-floor offices were designated for the auditor, recorder, treasurer, assessor, sheriff, and surveyor. The *Las Vegas Age* described the second-floor courtroom as its "crowning feature . . . [that] occupies the commanding position in the front center of the building . . . being also the monumental feature of the exterior by reason of the colonnade of Corinthian columns which encloses the front."[5] The room was to be 36 x 45 feet with a 22-foot ceiling.

On December 10, 1913, the county contracted with Campbell and Turner of Sacramento to build the courthouse for $46,400. Additional work by Savage Heating and Plumbing of Reno boosted the price to over $50,000. Under the supervision of L. J. Turner and H. S. Holt of Campbell and Turner, groundbreaking occurred on January 22, 1914. The railroad facilitated the construction by providing "a spur to the site of the building" to deliver materials efficiently.[6]

Although the contractors were supposed to complete the courthouse by July 1, 1914, county officials did not dedicate it until December 7 of that year. Just as many local newspapers did on such occasions throughout Nevada history, the *Las Vegas Age* boasted:

No public building in the state of Nevada, is more perfect in its architectural features or more beautiful in its interior fittings and furnishings than this new court house. Moreover, it is doubtful if any public building ever constructed in the state of Nevada has furnished more value for the expenditure than this.[7]

During the opening ceremonies, DeLongchamps received a standing ovation and was asked to address the gathering. His response was that "oratory [was] not in his line and that he preferred

The Clark County Courthouse and its park-like setting provided the community with an important focal point. The county demolished the building after completing its replacement in the late 1950s. (Photo ca. 1920; courtesy of the Alicia Lawrence Collection, James R. Dickinson Library, University of Nevada, Las Vegas)

to let the building he had designed speak for him."[8] Additional remarks were supplied by the Honorable Errol James L. Taber, judge of the district court. More prepared than the architect for the occasion, he touched on several topics, including "a plea to parents to watch over and care for their children and to preserve them so far as possible from the vice of gambling," ironic words indeed for Las Vegas was to become the world's gaming capital.[9] In 1914, however, Las Vegas was a railroad town, not a tourist mecca, and the *Las Vegas Age* article celebrating the courthouse opening included closing remarks on the importance of the transportation industry that "pays approximately two-thirds of all taxes collected by the county."[10]

In the 1930s, in the midst of the Great Depression, the state stumbled upon the ingredients of a boom that had nothing to do with mining, ranching, or railroads—the past major components of its economy. Liberal divorce and gambling laws built new industries that became critical in the shaping of Nevada's future. The gaming industry, in particular, at times seemed almost limitless, and as it grew so did the state's major urban centers. And of course, larger populations created a need for expanded county governments.[11]

Clark County, because of its explosive growth, initiated the state's most recent phase of courthouse construction.[12] In 1958 local architects Walter Zick and Harris Sharp designed the new Clark County Courthouse and set the tone for the era. The initial phase of construction placed the new facility next to the old DeLongchamps courthouse, with plans for the expansion of the new to eventually replace the old. The 1958 glass, concrete, and steel structure soars seven stories in the unadorned uniformity of the International style of architecture. It is an imposing building decorated in powder blue and stands in stark contrast to the ornate DeLongchamps courthouse that for a time was located to the rear.

A broad range of choices exist within any fashion of architecture. The International style can be used to create monumental buildings or functional offices and houses. Above all, the 1958 Clark County Courthouse was designed to be functional. The county's increasing needs dictated the building's size: A growing staff required a large facility. Nevertheless, large does not always mean monumental, and the courthouse lacked such features as a grand ceremonial entrance. The Clark County Courthouse belongs to a period when county governments were clothing themselves in practical garments.[13]

This contrasts with the private architecture of the city. Evaluating the effect of casino design on the community, author-architect Robert Venturi flamboyantly suggests that Las Vegas

The 1958 Clark County Courthouse was designed by Walter Zick and Harris Sharp in the International style. (Photo ca. 1960; courtesy of Clark County and the Nevada Historical Society)

is "our Florence . . . the Flamingo sign will be the model to shock our sensibilities towards a new architecture."[14] In the last half of the twentieth century, the community's buildings have exploded with new and fabulous creativity. They and their signs assume forms that exceed the lexicons of the architectural historian. As author Tom Wolfe suggests in his bizarrely titled book *The Kandy-Kolored Tangerine-Flake Streamline Baby*, these new images from Las Vegas are perhaps best described as "Boomerang Modern, Palette Curvilinear, Flash Gordon Ming-Alert Spiral, McDonald's Hamburger Parabola, Mint Casino Elliptical, Miami Beach Kidney."[15] Thomas Hine combines them under the term *Populuxe*, intended to signify the futuristic, sleek images of the 1950s and early 1960s.[16] Perhaps no community excelled more in the application of these images than Las Vegas.

Populuxe architecture became fashionable in the late 1950s and 1960s, just as Las Vegas assumed the first of many personae that would make it internationally famous. At the same time, the county erected a quiet, restrained courthouse, which in the context of Nevada is only remarkable as a public building for its size. It speaks eloquently of a time when Las Vegas left the creation of an architectural community symbol to the private sector. After all, the business world was feeding on a designing and building frenzy, which could not easily be matched at public expense.

In many ways, the Clark County Courthouse was the foremost expression of this era's public architecture in Nevada. Its design was a consequence of its use not its symbolism. The size of Clark County and its governmental services necessitated an imposing structure, making the courthouse the largest in the state. In spite of its size, however, the building was devoid of monumental scale. Its role was not intended as a community focal point. The Clark County Courthouse provided efficient, practical shelter for expanding governmental services. It lacked a symbolic statement about the role of government and the judicial court in the community.

As if in an attempt to counter the mundane origin and nature of courthouse architecture,

Clark County officials later initiated a plan to remodel the 1958 building. In the 1980s they funded the construction of a two-story concrete addition and colonnade around the courthouse. This included the massive, scored concrete blocks in the architectural style of Brutalism, a name that does not denote a value judgment. The popularity of the term is probably derived from its association with Peter Smithson, an architect who specialized in the style after World War I and whose face reminded his friends of ancient Rome's busts of Brutus.[17] The selection of this style

Remodeling and additions to the Clark County Courthouse provide a good example of Brutalist architecture. (Ronald M. James)

for the addition to the Clark County Courthouse contrasts with the plain, almost futuristic metal and glass lines of the core structure. The remodeling gave an air of public architecture to the building, and it took the courthouse a step beyond its original practical design.

If it is true, as Venturi suggests, that Las Vegas is the architectural vanguard of the nation, it is clear that it did not get there by preserving older buildings, no matter how distinguished they might be. The 1914 Spanish Colonial Revival courthouse was demolished after being replaced in 1958, making Clark County the only local government to have discarded a DeLongchamps courthouse. The original 1909 concrete-block Clark County Courthouse was also gone by then. After ceasing to function as a courthouse, it served as a city hall and library, and was finally removed in the early 1950s.

The construction, demolition, and modification of the Clark County courthouses are unique in Nevada. In less than eighty years, the local government erected three courthouses and gave a major facelift to its last. No other Nevada county has attempted to update its architectural image as frequently or to provide for services that have expanded as dramatically.[18]

5 : DOUGLAS COUNTY

In 1865 as the new state of Nevada helped the nation celebrate the end of the Civil War, the people of tiny Genoa completed their first courthouse. It was a substantial brick structure, one of the first of its kind in the state, and it seemed to reflect the wishes of all that it be permanent. Today it remains as the oldest standing courthouse in Nevada. In 1916 a DeLongchamps-designed courthouse in Minden replaced the Genoa facility, but where there was change there was also continuity. Together, the two courthouses erected by Douglas County officials are strong examples of an architecture for a stable, prosperous, but small agricultural community.

Traders from Utah founded Genoa in 1851, originally calling it Mormon Station. The town

The Douglas County Courthouse in Genoa is the oldest surviving county building in the state. One of the few brick structures in town at the time, it stood prominently on the west side of Main Street in this photograph taken before fire gutted it in 1910. (Nevada Historical Society)

became the government seat for Carson County of the Utah Territory in 1854. Situated at the foot of the eastern slope of the Sierra in Carson Valley, it was an ideal way station for westbound pioneers in desperate need of supplies and fresh teams. The lush flood plain was unusually suitable for agriculture in the western Great Basin. In 1861 the Nevada territorial legislature designated Mormon Station—by then usually called Genoa—as the seat of the newly created Douglas County, one of the original nine. They named it after Stephen A. Douglas, the Democratic candidate for President in 1860 and Lincoln's opponent in the famous 1858 debates on the expansion of slavery. Douglas served as chairman of the U.S. Senate Committee of Territories until he died the same year the county was organized.

Because of its long history as a territorial county seat, Genoa faced the problem of accommodating its courts for several years. In 1860 President Buchanan appointed John Cradlebaugh judge of the second judicial district of the western portion of the Utah Territory, but the judge's "courthouse" did little to inspire a feeling that civilization had arrived on the frontier. According to Myron Angel, his hall of justice was a livery stable made of clapboard, repaired and furnished for $750. He wrote: "In the upper part of the building Judge Cradlebaugh held his first United States District Court, access to it being had through the front door by means of a ladder from the street."[1] Cradlebaugh's accommodations matched the primitive nature of the settlement. One account maintains that when he assumed the bench, "the town was filled to overflowing with lawyers, litigants, witnesses, and jurors. A bundle of straw in a barn was eagerly sought as a bed, and the judge slept contentedly between rival attorneys, while humbler attendants spread their blankets on the sage-brush."[2] During the following months, the seat of justice was shuttled from one inadequate hall to another. Angel further points out that the first Douglas County commission, which met in 1862, found that because

the old Carson County Court House was not in condition to warrant fitting up for a continuation in its old line of service, they decided to pay J. S. Child thirty dollars for one month's rent for a building for that purpose. They also decided to rent "the cell" in the old Reese mill and fit it up for a jail.[3]

It would be several years before a judge at Genoa presided in a formal courthouse. A rented structure satisfied the immediate need for shelter, and dignity could come later.

In 1864 the Nevada territorial government authorized the Douglas County commission to tax property owners for the construction of a courthouse—the cost of which was "not to exceed the sum of twenty thousand dollars."[4] T. J. Furbee, Superintendent of the Sierra Silver Mining, Saw and Quartz Mill Company provided architectural services to the county for its new building project. Furbee was part of an unsuccessful effort to create a profitable mining district north of Genoa. As with many of the state's small communities, Genoa probably lacked people with architectural training but did have the talent from the mining industry needed to erect substantial structures.

Furbee's design for Douglas County called for a two-story vernacular brick structure with Greek Revival elements. It had a courtroom on the second floor and a jail in the rear of the first. The plans also called for a sturdy stone foundation 3 feet below the surface, $2\frac{1}{2}$-feet thick. Furbee requested $125 for his services but was awarded $100 by the county commissioners.

A contemporary account points out that the county jail consisted of six cells, each 6 x 8 feet. Furbee's specifications provided security for the cells with 2-foot-thick walls and a ceiling of $1\frac{1}{2}$-inch rough plank sheathed with $\frac{1}{8}$-inch sheet iron. His specifications further asserted that "the seams are to be well riveted to the plank with washers on the upper side. And the Court Room floor over the cells to be lined with the same kind of iron."[5]

The 66 x 36-foot structure—small by today's standards—included ample room for offices, jury rooms, and judicial chambers. With a 12-foot-high ceiling on the first floor and 14-foot-high rooms on the second level, the courthouse has the vertical appearance typical of monumental architecture of the period. A central staircase provides access between floors.

Tin covered the wooden roof. A contemporary newspaper account points out that "a wooden cornice, a ten inch projection with heavy scroll brackets, sets off the building very tastefully."[6] Monumental twin doors, 10 feet tall, provided the main entrance to the building. The plans included details for the courtroom: "There is to be a Judge's stand four . . . feet wide, and six . . . feet long. The platform to be two feet and six inches high and to show a panel front:

The 1865 Douglas County jail in Genoa was an iron box with doors. It had a bleak interior and little ventilation. (Nevada Historical Society)

there is to be a railing across the Bar of four . . . inch turned banisters with two gates to correspond."[7]

Local contractors Lawrence Gilman and L. C. Chapman began work on the structure in April 1865. During the course of the construction, Gilman purchased the interest of Chapman and formed an association with Rufus Adams, a prominent rancher who had settled in Carson Valley in the early 1850s. His brother, John Quincy Adams, supplied brick for the courthouse as he later did for the U.S. Mint building in Carson City.[8] Gilman and Adams finished the project in October 1865. Since the structure still stands, it appears that Furbee was a competent designer and that the county employed capable builders.

Despite overruns, the total cost of the courthouse in Genoa did not exceed $20,000. The *Douglas County Banner* pointed out that "the entire building is hand finished throughout except the portion occupied by the jail . . . The entire edifice is fire-proof, having iron doors and shutters to each opening."[9] It served as the courthouse for forty-five years while the seat remained in Genoa.

Fire raged through the town and gutted the building on June 28, 1910. The county rushed through a restoration project that cost about $18,000 and was completed on December 27, 1910, probably in an attempt to quell any call for a move of the seat of government. Still, some people began to question Genoa's suitability. Growth elsewhere had worked against the tiny hamlet because it was no longer an important pioneer way station, and the twin farming towns of Gardnerville and Minden to the east were booming. Local, powerful families had established the communities in a central location in the valley to provide services to agricultural industries. When the Virginia & Truckee Railroad reached Minden in 1906, it assured the importance of the twin towns as a mercantile center. The valuable role Genoa played at the foot of the Sierra, as a resting point for overland travelers, had become an anachronism. By promising to advocate the construction of a high school in Gardnerville, civic leaders in Minden managed to gain its sister community's support for a county-seat shift, which became official on January 1, 1916. After the relocation of government, until 1956, the Genoa Courthouse served as an elementary school. Since 1969 it has been used as a local museum, and during that time the community renovated the building. Although it has undergone many changes, it is still possible to discern Furbee's simple, forceful design.

In anticipation of the move to Minden, county commissioners secured the services of DeLongchamps and his associate, George L. F. O'Brien, to design a new courthouse. In contrast with its Genoa predecessor, his plan, accepted on May 6, 1915, called for a conservative Neo-Classical building with a horizontal emphasis. DeLongchamps received approximately $700 for

The renovated 1865 Douglas County Courthouse now serves as a local museum. (Ronald M. James)

his efforts. Contractors Friedhoff and Hoeffel quickly constructed the new courthouse and had it ready for the grand opening on New Year's Day of 1916.[10] The building cost Douglas County approximately $25,000. Situated on an oversized landscaped lot in Minden's residential district, the courthouse setting is one of the more tranquil in the state.

In spite of the subsequent modifications, the Douglas County Courthouse remains as an elegant example of the work of DeLongchamps. The single-story structure rests on a raised concrete basement and has a flat roof banded by a low-brick parapet with a concrete cap. A dentil cornice with full entablature is found beneath the parapet. The walls are clad in beige-colored brick. The front elevation includes an open concrete staircase that ascends to a recessed entry supported by four columns. Simple twin-brick pilasters accent the building on both sides of the portico. The building plan provides for an entry hall leading to the glass and wooden doors of the courtroom and a longer hall that forms the central axis of the building with access to the county offices.[11] The hallways are decorated with black marble wainscoting, adding to the distinguished character of the structure. The *Record-Courier* of Douglas County boasted that "the court room is said to be one of the finest of its kind in the state. It is particularly well lighted and arranged and embraces all of the modern conveniences found in an up-to-date court room." It also stated that the building was "a splendid example of architecture and carries with it the dignity that bespeaks for the progressiveness of the people of Douglas County."[12]

Space was set aside in the basement for a jury room, several other rooms, and a two-cell prison so well built that "the sheriff or his assistants can lock up or unlock prisoners without going into the jail." The *Record-Courier* further observed that there were plans for the installation of another cell for women "but judging from the past history of Douglas County [it] will be seldom used. Only one woman has occupied the county jail in a period of twenty-five years."[13] In all, the new Douglas County Courthouse captures a time when the Progressive movement dominated the nation's politics. Stressing responsible, corruption-free government, the Progressives were at their zenith when Douglas County planned its new facility. Correspondingly, the courthouse is understated in its scale and presentation. It depicts a government that is sturdy, in balance, and well founded, but not self-possessed and overly grandiose or pompous.

DeLongchamps designed an addition for the north side of the courthouse in 1956. The 20 x 42-foot two-story annex included space for a juvenile cell and for the sheriff's and assessor's offices. In 1964 the county employed the Reno architectural firm of Ferris, Erskine, and Calef to design a 6,000-square-foot addition to the south side of the building, which cost $174,245. Even though the additions sacrificed the symmetry of the building, they were compatible with the original design and merely exaggerated its already horizontal appearance.

DeLongchamps designed the Neo-Classical Douglas County Courthouse, which opened in Minden on January 1, 1916, with elegant Ionic columns. (Ronald M. James)

6 : ELKO COUNTY

The major population centers of the state, Virginia City, Goldfield, Reno, and recently Las Vegas, have always been closely tied to the Nevada-California border, and each have served for a time as the state's largest city. As the most northeastern county seat, Elko is as removed as any major community in the state from Nevada's heaviest population centers. As a result, it has consistently sought to establish a separate, distinct identity. The citizens of Elko have constructed two distinguished county buildings, and the history of this public architecture reflects the place's isolation.

The state legislature created Elko County in March 1869 because the town of Elko had suddenly sprung to life as a stop on the transcontinental railroad and as an extension of regional cattle-grazing areas. Far removed from Austin, the seat of Lander County that had encompassed all of northeastern Nevada, Elko needed its own governmental administration. Elko County commissioners initially secured temporary accommodations, occupying three adobe structures and a tent. Within months they quickly set themselves to the task of building a courthouse. They selected a site one block from the business district and awarded local builder Colonel W. P. Monroe a contract for $17,444 to begin the work. The county hired Dan P. Bell, who was later to serve as the architect of the Lander County Courthouse, to supervise the project.[1] The Elko County Courthouse, designed by Walter Moberly, included a formal adaptation of classical details.[2] Moberly was born in England around 1833, and at the time of the construction of the courthouse, he served as county surveyor.[3] The *Elko Independent* reported that the courthouse

> is to be forty by sixty feet, two stories high, and of the Roman Doric style of architecture. On the first or lower floor there will be four rooms for offices . . . with a fire proof vault in one; and also on this floor five cells for holding prisoners, nine by ten feet. On the second floor will be the courtroom at one end of the building, thirty by sixty feet, and four offices . . . and a portico in the front eight feet in width.[4]

As Monroe began construction, however, some individuals called for a more elaborate design. The *Elko Independent* pointed out that a few alterations could be made, which would cost little and yet would improve the appearance of the structure. The newspaper further asserted: "As the building is designed for permanent use, there can be nothing lost to the tax-payers to have it erected in a style commensurate with the importance of our growing county."[5] The commissioners followed the newspaper's suggestions and altered the original design to include higher walls, a heavy cornice, and changes in the front steps. In spite of these alterations, Monroe finished the brick courthouse on December 18, 1869, in less than four months. Elko was the first county to build during the second era of courthouse construction in Nevada. Monroe and county officials subsequently disagreed over the final bill. After paying him $22,250, the commissioners

The 1869 Elko County Courthouse was one of the state's finest Greek Revival structures. It served as an important part of the community until its demolition in 1910. (Nevada Historical Society)

rejected his claim for an additional $240 for locks. Failing to be reimbursed, Monroe duplicated the keys to the courthouse and distributed them throughout Elko, forcing the county to replace the locks at a cost of $600.[6] The building was formally accepted on December 22, 1869.

The Elko County Courthouse exhibited a degree of elegance that went beyond the vernacular structures of the previous era. While Elko was a long way from Carson City and Washington, D.C., it appears that its citizens wished to demonstrate that they were in the cultural mainstream. Although the design references to Greek Revival architecture were becoming increasingly old-fashioned by 1869, the Elko County Courthouse was, nevertheless, a well-planned building with something more than a haphazard application of a nationally accepted form of architecture. Moberly's training is unknown, but his building clearly demonstrates his talent for design.

In 1910 Elko County commissioners voted to build a new, larger courthouse. William H. Weeks, a prominent California architect, provided the design, which employed ornate details from the Neo-Classical style. Weeks was born in 1866 on Prince Edward Island, Canada, and came to the United States in 1886.[7] His two-story structure, situated on the site of its predecessor, cost $150,000. Following the demolition of the older facility, the county conducted a cornerstone-laying ceremony on August 2, 1910.[8] The Sellman Brothers of Reno constructed the symmetrical nine-bay courthouse. The building has a two-story pedimented portico supported by four Tuscan-style columns with stylized Doric capitals. An ornate balustrade follows the roof line and accentuates a cornice with full entablature. The building is supported by a raised masonry foundation and is crowned by a flat roof and a shallow dome. Heavy terra cotta cornerstones, or quoins, decorate the building's walls. Originally quoins were larger structural elements that held the corners of a building together. By the time of the construction of the Elko County Courthouse, quoining had become decorative, merely imitating the appearance of a necessary building component. The image of Lady Justice's face decorates the principal elevation above the door in bas-relief.

The structure initiated a trend that DeLongchamps's courthouse designs would continue for the rest of the decade—contemporary architectural styles in professional, traditional ways contrasting with many of the state's nineteenth-century public buildings. In 1916 an article in the "Industrial Issue" of the *Elko Independent* boasted, as local papers often did on such an occasion, that the courthouse "isn't the State Capitol, as many might suppose, at first glance. It is

William H. Weeks designed the still-extant 1911 Elko County Courthouse as a highly ornate Neo-Classical building with a shallow dome and a balustrade along the roof-line. (Photo by M. F. Jukes, 1914; courtesy of the Nevada Historical Society)

the beautiful $150,000 county courthouse . . . built for the needs of the present." The same article maintained that local leaders anticipated needing to replace it within twenty years, to keep pace with the quickly growing county.[9] In spite of the prediction, the county has never found it necessary to move from the facility even in the face of Elko's mining boom of the late twentieth century.

The courtroom of the 1911 Elko County Courthouse was built in a grand style that rivaled any of the contemporary DeLongchamps structures. (Nevada Historical Society)

7 : ESMERALDA COUNTY

Esmeralda County, on the California border between Carson City and Las Vegas, has had three seats of government, only one of which is within its current boundaries. The county constructed two courthouses, each reflecting distinct periods of its history. Because the first building in Esmeralda County, constructed as a courthouse, served two local governments, it is more fully discussed in Chapter 13. The second, more recent courthouse is the monumental turn-of-the-century structure in Goldfield. Its rough-hewn stone façade captures the rustic primitive quality of one of Nevada's last mining boomtowns.

Esmeralda County was organized in 1861 with its first seat of government in Aurora—a mining town perched high in the Sierra near the California border. According to Angel, the county leased, and later purchased, a brick building on the corner of Pine and Silver Streets.[1] California authorities from Mono County erected a jail in Aurora during the time when the two states disputed the jurisdiction of the town, and Esmeralda County officials used it until 1874 when they built a new jail facility in the courthouse.

When the fortunes of Aurora declined, commissioners moved their government down the mountain to Hawthorne—a railroad town with a stable economy. This occurred with little dispute when the state legislature passed an act on July 1, 1883, to authorize the move. As so often happened during the early period of local government in Nevada, officials had not built a courthouse in the county seat. Without public construction funds invested in Aurora, the move was easy to justify. At the foot of the eastern slope of the Sierra, Hawthorne was division headquarters for the Carson & Colorado Railway. As in the case of Reno, Elko, and Winnemucca, the railroad not only created a sizeable community, but it also provided a mantle of permanence that a mining town had difficulty claiming. Shortly after the county-seat move to Hawthorne, local government officials completed the construction of the well-designed brick courthouse. The structure served the county until 1907 when the seat of government relocated once again, this time to the boisterous, young mining boomtown of Goldfield to the south.

Goldfield is an example of a meteoric success story in Nevada history. For a short time after the turn of the century, it became the state's largest city, and Hawthorne, now a small community, itself fell easy victim to a government-seat shift. The county government, however, was one of Hawthorne's only viable industries. In addition, county officials had invested considerable funds into the construction of the courthouse that was barely twenty years old. Some even argued that Goldfield, as a mining boomtown, had an uncertain fate, while Hawthorne, though smaller, boasted a stable foundation and proven record.

The residents of Goldfield, nevertheless, pushed for county seat removal. The first attempt failed during the 1905 legislative session. After that defeat, the residents of Goldfield petitioned the Esmeralda County commission for a special election to vote on the move. The commission rejected the proposal, claiming that the effort did not include sufficient signatures. The 1907 legislature reviewed the issue again, and for several weeks it dominated the session. Public hearings and debates raged, but despite protests from the residents of Hawthorne, the legislature authorized the move of the government seat to Goldfield, effective on May 1, 1907.[2]

Construction on a new Esmeralda County Courthouse began immediately. In July 1907 commissioners awarded a contract of almost $80,000 to John Shea of Salt Lake City. Shea completed the structure so quickly that county officials were able to occupy it in 1908.

In the midst of the courthouse construction, Goldfield was immersed in the most important labor upheaval in the history of the state. Strikes and disputes between the mine owners and the

THE COURT HOUSE
AT GOLDFIELD, NEVADA

The 1907 Esmeralda County Courthouse in Goldfield exhibits Mission Revival features in its stone-block construction. (Photo ca. 1950; courtesy of the Nevada Historical Society)

Industrial Workers of the World and Western Federation of Miners dominated the community between 1906 and 1908. In December 1907 Governor Sparks requested the presence of federal troops on the prompting from mine owners. Many have criticized the action as unneeded. Whether warranted or indefensible, the outcome was clear: The intimidating federal presence effectively broke the union movement.[3]

The conflict furnished the backdrop for the erection of one of the harshest courthouse façades built in Nevada. Its massive entrance is crowned with an overhanging eave. A tall-stepped parapet with the name of the building and the date of its construction looms above the doorway and rises to castle-like heights at the courthouse's four corners, making it look like a fortress. The roughly finished stone of its façade adds to its medieval appearance as do the battlement-like parapets at the corners of the building.[4] The two-story, 75-foot-wide by 85-foot-deep square building design included a first-floor central hall, with offices for county officials and a staircase to the second-floor courtroom, district judge and attorney offices, and jury and commissioners rooms. The interior was finished in yellow pine with battleship-gray paint and had linoleum floors. A basement provided space for storage and a furnace. A 30 x 50-foot jail extends to the rear.[5]

Although the architecture of the Esmeralda County Courthouse might be regarded as an abstract adaptation of Mission Revival, this mining-town courthouse does not seem to reflect any particular style of architecture. The symbolism of law and order outweighs any hint of an architectural centerpiece for the community or an expression of civilization that might have been intended. The county built the courthouse as a fortress either because the leadership itself felt under siege or as a remarkable coincidence of the current events and public architecture. The exact cause and effect relationship of labor upheaval and courthouse design appears lost in an undocumented past. Nevertheless, the courthouse can serve as a symbol of a pivotal period in

Nevada's history. After all, this courthouse has all the coldness of a remote Western federal penitentiary.

Ultimately, those residents of Hawthorne who claimed that the fortunes of Goldfield might turn were proven correct. The mines declined within a decade and Nevada's largest city was soon to become one of its smallest county seats. Today, the county government is one of the community's major industries.

8 : EUREKA COUNTY

Eureka County in central Nevada is home to one of the state's most elegant nineteenth-century courthouses. Modest when compared with the contemporaneous Storey County Courthouse, the Eureka facility is nevertheless substantial and well designed, and it expresses in architecture the spirit of a community tied to a relatively stable but limited economy.

Prospectors discovered extensive silver-lead ore deposits and established the Eureka Mining District on September 19, 1864. Never the location of an explosively spectacular mining boom on the scale of California's gold country or Nevada's Comstock, the district, nevertheless, had mineral deposits that promised consistent rewards. The Greek word *eureka*, "I have found it," is a popular place name throughout the mining West, but its application here, of all places, is ironic because the discoveries hardly warranted such elation.

Throughout the late 1860s and early 1870s, the district's population grew gradually until the lawmakers decided to carve a new county from the eastern portion of Lander County. The legislature created Eureka County on March 1, 1873. Resentment over county-seat shifts and divisions has been common in the history of Nevada, but this was apparently not the case between Lander and Eureka Counties. For example, a contemporary article in the *Reese River Reveille*, the Lander County newspaper, printed the following benediction over its new neighbor: "May your treasury be plethoric and your jail vacuous; may the blessing of a wise, beneficent and economical government be and abide with you now and forever, Amen."[1]

Eureka County officials took precautions to make certain that their treasury would not be empty, an approach endorsed by the local newspaper. An editorial in the *Eureka Sentinel* pointed out that "it has been the universal rule in this State to plunge new counties into almost hopeless indebtedness." The editorial went on to suggest that "We should not get high-toned until we can afford it."[2] Perhaps with this in mind, the county commissioners were slow to build a courthouse.

Thanks to the donation of a building, the county avoided costly new construction. On March 25, 1873, the Eureka County commissioners accepted a skating rink on Main and Bateman Streets and converted it into a public building. Donated by Judge John O. Darrow, it was the perfect solution for a frugal local government.[3] The lot, valued at $4,000, was 40 x 100 feet. Predictably, modifications to the structure were necessary. The county built a formidable jail at the rear and altered the interior of the courthouse. According to Virginia City's *Territorial Enterprise*, the jail floor was composed of "two by six scantling spiked together sidewise, and laid on the edge, making, with the thickness of the timber and the number of spikes, an almost impenetrable mass of wood and iron." The newspaper went on to point out that "the County Jail will be rather diminutive in size, but will be unsurpassed in point of structure."[4] Plans for the jail show a cross section of the facility with a complex locking system for four metal doors.[5] The jail remained in use until the 1980s. Throughout the summer of 1873 work progressed within the courthouse on a vault for county records "as nearly fire-proof as a construction of the kind can well be made."[6] The county purchased doors in Hamilton, the county seat of White Pine County, where they were formerly used in a bank.

Although fires and floods repeatedly devastated the community in its early years, its makeshift courthouse served for over six years. Shortly before it was abandoned it nearly fell victim to one of Eureka's greatest fires. The disaster that swept through the town on the night of April 18, 1879, destroying hundreds of structures, reminded people of the vulnerability of their old wooden county building, and it probably verified for many that its replacement was in order.[7] Three days later, anticipating new construction, the county sold the skating-rink courthouse, which the new owner apparently moved from the property in the month that followed. Whether the structure is extant is unknown.

Clearly by 1879 Eureka was ready to become a little more high toned. The county commissioners reviewed at least three designs presented by different architects. The preservation of the optional plans in the Eureka County Courthouse provides one of the most outstanding opportunities from nineteenth-century Nevada to understand how a commission settled on a style of architecture.[8] Among these are the plans of George F. Costerisan, who won the contract, as well as proposals by C. M. Bennett and W. H. Bayless. Little is known about Bayless except that he claimed to be an architect. Bennett was the designer of the impressive Fourth Ward School of Virginia City, constructed in 1875–1877, but as with Bayless, additional information on his life is unavailable.[9]

Costerisan was a native of Pennsylvania, born on February 5, 1846. When still young, he moved to Wisconsin with his family. He was a Civil War veteran and received some education at the Kimball Institute in Baraboo, Wisconsin. He apprenticed with a local architect named Palmer for one year and then with C. P. Randall of Chicago for two more years. He supervised the construction of the Algona County Courthouse in Iowa and later opened an office in Decorah, Iowa. From this central location, he designed buildings in Wisconsin, Iowa, and Minnesota until 1878 when he moved to Eureka, Nevada. It was shortly after his move that he submitted his plans for the Eureka County Courthouse.[10] He was clearly one of the most trained and experienced architects to practice in Nevada during the nineteenth century.

Bayless's design called for a formal, symmetrical, Greek Revival courthouse with a pedimented front gable, a dentil cornice, and tall pilasters with ornate caps. Nationwide, the Greek Revival style was outmoded and had been little used for about twenty years. The four-over-four pane windows with pedimented and segmented caps and a balcony over the main entrance displayed a more contemporary influence with its Italianate motifs. Although long used in American public architecture, the clock tower can also be called Italianate and was out of step with the overall Greek Revival design. In short, Bayless's proposal awkwardly combined elements of diverse styles.

Bennett's proposal called for an ornate Italianate structure, reminiscent of the Storey County Courthouse designed by the San Francisco firm Kenitzer and Raun and built in 1875–1877. Since Bennett was in Virginia City during the time, working on the Fourth Ward School, it is possible that the plans of the prestigious California firm influenced him. Bennett's design employed motifs found on the Storey County building, including ornate metal window surrounds, pilasters, cornice, an ornamental cornice cap with the date of construction, a porch, and finials.

Although Costerisan was awarded the contract, a complete set of his designs is nonexistent. Approved plans become the builder's working drawings and are most susceptible to loss through use. Ultimately, his building can be seen as a uniformly Italianate version of much of the Bayless

The 1879 plans proposed by W. H. Bayless for a Greek Revival courthouse in Eureka were never used. The Italianate cupola (above the roof) and the balcony above the door deviate from traditional Greek Revival architecture. (Ronald M. James)

The 1879 plans proposed by C. M. Bennett for a courthouse in Eureka exhibited Italianate style architecture and were never used. (Ronald M. James)

proposal. For example, the window treatment, the porch and the main entry, and the idea for tall pilasters between bays are identical to the Bayless plan. Perhaps the Eureka County commissioners were impressed with Costerisan but asked him to incorporate features from Bayless's design. The exact process, however, is lost from the historical record. Of more interest is the way local taste and preference contributed to design.

When confronted with a similar choice, the Storey County commissioners picked the most ornate design of the three options they had. The Eureka County commissioners, however,

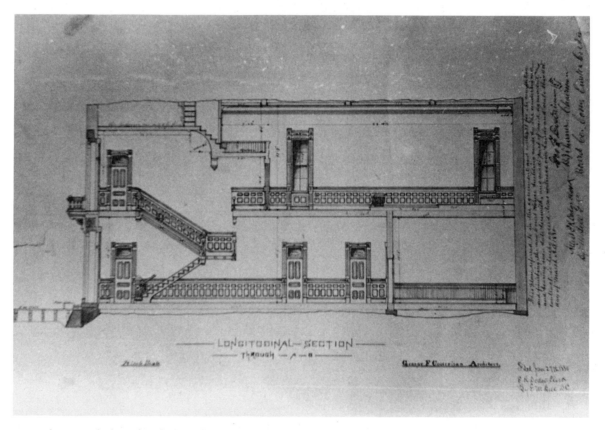

Several optional plans for the Eureka County Courthouse were carefully preserved by the county. Unfortunately, this cross section of the courthouse is all that survives of Costerisan's initial proposal. The simple contemporary structure continues to serve as a courthouse. (Ronald M. James)

rejected the one with elaborate ironwork and ornamentation. They also rejected the out-of-date Greek Revival proposal and settled, instead, on the simpler contemporary plan developed by or with Costerisan. Comparison of the alternative sets of plans preserved in the Eureka County Courthouse make it clear that the county commissioners decided to avoid heavy ornamentation in favor of simplicity.

The selected design called for a structure that was larger than the donated lot of the original facility, necessitating county acquisition and use of the neighboring land. R. Ryland began

The Eureka County Courthouse remains as one of two nineteenth-century courthouses still in use in Nevada. (Ronald M. James)

construction on the courthouse in June 1879. He completed the exterior within the year and then gave up the contract. Costerisan finished the interior, at which point the county hired J. S. Whitton to supervise the work. On June 3, 1880, the county commissioners accepted the courthouse, which cost about $38,000.[11] The vault and other fixtures boosted the price over $50,000.[12] The building remains as one of two nineteenth-century Nevada structures still in use as a courthouse. The two-story brick courthouse measures 50 x 80 feet and rises an imposing 51 feet above Main Street. The Costerisan design called for a central door on both floors, opening to the principal elevation and flanked on each side by two windows. The pediments of the first-floor windows are triangular while those above are segmented. A balcony supported by brackets shades the Main Street entrance. Heavy boiler-plate shutters manufactured by John R. Simms of San Francisco can close over each window in case of fire. Brick pilasters provide an accent for the front façade that rises to a metal, bracketed cornice and parapet wall with detailed brick work. The roof is clad in tin.

The interior includes a large hall and staircase. A Spanish cedar balustrade accents other natural woods and gilded details throughout the interior. Costerisan designed the main floor for the district attorney's office with an adjoining counsel room. On the opposite side of the hall was space for the county recorder with a vault. The architect also set aside room for the county assessor and treasurer. In the northwest corner of the main floor, connected to the old jail, was an office for the sheriff. The second floor included office space for the judge and the county clerk, and a vault. Swinging doors afford entry to the courtroom, one of the best preserved from the nineteenth century in Nevada. Roughly 45 feet square, the room rises 19 feet to a pressed metal ceiling, and it has a gallery suspended at the rear, with room for one hundred seats. The witness box, placed directly in front of the judge's bench, is a large semicircle, distinctive for its shape and place. Interestingly, the ornamentation of a clock, purchased by the county in 1873, influenced Costerisan's plan for the interior. For several years the clock hung in the adapted skating-rink

The nineteenth-century courtroom of the Eureka County Courthouse is one of the best preserved in Nevada. An elaborate pressed-metal ceiling is matched by extensive woodwork, and the clock, purchased in 1873, has carved details duplicated in the building's interior ornamentation. (Ronald M. James)

courthouse and it must have been regarded as a valuable possession because Costerisan used its woodwork as a pattern for the interior ornamentation throughout the county's new facility.

The *Eureka Sentinel* completed its description of the new courthouse at the opening of the facility by pointing out that "the building is well lighted and ventilated; with a good water supply in each room. It is also fitted for gas." McNally and Hawkins of San Francisco provided the plumbing materials, and William Robertson completed the painting and graining—paint applied in such a way to make less expensive woods look like oak or walnut.[13]

After the completion of the courthouse, Costerisan moved to San Francisco where he opened a dry goods store and prospected for gold. He eventually returned to architecture, designing schools, churches, and commercial structures in Eureka, California. From 1886 to 1890 he practiced in Los Angeles after which he moved to Salt Lake City and designed three schools. In 1894 he returned to Los Angeles. Of his many structures, perhaps none is more impressive than the Eureka County Courthouse.

Fittingly, the *Eureka Sentinel* claimed shortly after its completion that "there is but one finer [courthouse] . . . in the state, that of Storey County, which cost more than three times as much as ours."[14] Lambert Molinelli, a local booster, went further by suggesting that the courthouse was "one of the finest county buildings on the coast and will certainly be a matter of laudable pride to all citizens of the county."[15] Molinelli's prediction still holds true.

9 : HUMBOLDT COUNTY

Humboldt County erected two courthouses, each intended to increase its prestige. The county, dating from 1861, originally encompassed much of the northwestern corner of the state. It takes its name from the Humboldt River, itself named by explorer John C. Frémont after Baron Friedrich Heinrich Alexander von Humboldt (1769–1859), the German geographer, map maker, and scientist. Because the county is large and situated on a key east-west corridor, its economy has depended on transportation, mining, and agricultural activities. Humboldt County encompassed emigrant trails and active mining districts that attracted much of its earlier population, but ranching and farming also played an increasingly important role. Thus, Unionville, Humboldt County's first county seat, was a mining town, and Winnemucca, its second, depended on agriculture and the railroad for economic survival. Unionville never built a courthouse, but Winnemucca quickly constructed a monumental public building.

Unionville was a mining boomtown in the 1860s when it claimed the seat for the new Humboldt County. Originally, government functions and the district court were established in an unsuitable local building. Later, in 1863, Sheriff Robert McBeth leased the Buena Vista Saloon for $60 a month.[1] The accommodations must have suited the booming community, as evidenced by the subsequent purchase of the structure by the county and by the fact that public officials remained in the facility for about ten years. Nevertheless, the semisubterranean building had several structural problems and became a source of humor for the local newspaper. The *Humboldt Register* pointed out that it

> is a fine place, except when it is dry and the sun beating upon the thin, flat roof; or when the snow is melting and dripping through; or when rain is falling, and the water coming down as through a ladder, all over the room.[2]

Still, the decision to house the county facilities in a bar had merit. The local saloon was often one of the earliest structures in a mining community and was also a kind of community center.

As the mines of Unionville declined in the late 1860s and early 1870s, the local newspaper began to call for construction of a courthouse. County government was the town's most viable industry and its loss would be devastating. Investing in a courthouse in Unionville could conceivably discourage a shift in the seat of government. The local newspaper proclaimed:

> The present Court House, designed originally as a saloon, is in no wise fitted for the purpose for which it is now used. We should have, and the resources of the county will justify it, buildings in which every citizen of the county will feel an honest pride in being a joint owner.[3]

Nevertheless, Unionville did not undertake the public construction project. A new dynamic community soon challenged the claim to the county government seat. By 1872 the Unionville mining district had seen its best days, while the railroad town of Winnemucca to the north grew. Clearly, the transcontinental railroad reshaped the map of Nevada. Like the contemporaneous Washoe County seat struggle that pitted Reno against Washoe City, political maneuvering and accusations of wrongdoing dominated the controversy in Humboldt County. Also, like Reno, Winnemucca took its case to the 1871 legislature, but while the lawmaking body decided in favor of Reno, it was divided over the case of Winnemucca; the senate voted in favor of the move, the assembly against it. In 1872 another attempt to encourage the county commissioners to move the seat to Winnemucca failed, but later that year a fire destroyed the courthouse and much of the business district, thus sealing Unionville's fate.[4] It was apparent to most that public funds for the construction of a new courthouse would be better spent elsewhere. In February 1873 the state legislature transferred the county seat to Winnemucca. Attempts to challenge the change in the courts proved unsuccessful, and the move became official.[5]

Humboldt County commissioners acted quickly to erect a courthouse and to secure their hold on the right to govern from Winnemucca. By 1874 Humboldt County had a new courthouse. James Z. Kelly, supervising architect for the Washoe County Courthouse, performed a similar function in Winnemucca. A contractor named Murphy from Stockton was responsible for the construction, which cost about $47,800.[6]

This, the first courthouse constructed in Humboldt County, was a rectangular brick building with modest Italianate details and included a second-story balcony over the main entrance, an octagonal cupola, a five-bay façade with elongated windows, interior side chimneys, and a pedimented gable orientated to the street. Its kinship to the earlier Kelly courthouse in Reno is clear from historic photographs (see the Washoe County Courthouse photographs in chapter 17). The building served the county until 1918 when it succumbed to fire.

Unlike the Unionville courthouse fire, the Winnemucca blaze posed little threat to the community's hold on local government.[7] Commissioners could proceed cautiously, first examining the possibility of rehabilitating the ruins. They later determined that a new structure was more practical, and so they followed that course methodically. To make certain that the new courthouse would be the best possible public building, the commissioners secured the services of

Humboldt County's first courthouse in Winnemucca was an Italianate structure built in 1874, which burned in 1918. (Nevada Historical Society)

DeLongchamps—by then a renowned Nevada architect who had demonstrated his architectural skills.

In 1919 DeLongchamps designed the plans for the new courthouse that, after revisions, came within the commissioners' limit of $150,000. Construction on the original courthouse site proceeded under the supervision of Lehman A. Ferris, who also assisted in the construction of the Humboldt Hotel and the local grammar school, all of the same period. Officials laid the cornerstone for the courthouse in February 1920, and after several delays, the courthouse opened on January 1, 1921.[8] DeLongchamps's design plans entailed a 90 x 90-foot building of Neo-Classical

DeLongchamps's Humboldt County Courthouse is a substantial, conservative adaptation of Neo-Classical architecture. The courthouse opened on January 1, 1921. (Kathryn M. Kuranda)

The staircase in the Humboldt County Courthouse is central to one of DeLongchamps's most monumental interiors. (Ronald M. James)

design, influenced by Beaux-Arts architecture. The impressive two-story structure is finished with buff-colored brick and cream-colored terra cotta. Corinthian columns support its pedimented portico. Matching brick pilasters, capped with terra cotta, divide the entrance wall into five bays, and there are eagles with wings outstretched to decorate the spaces above the doors on the main and north entries.

The Neo-Classical interior of the courthouse, DeLongchamps's most monumental, is one of the finest of its kind in the state. It includes a sweeping marble staircase and a two-story atrium decorated with Ionic columns and a lead-glass ceiling. The main-floor entrance supports square columns with ornate capitals and includes space for the treasurer, auditor, recorder, assessor, and surveyor. The second story has offices for the district attorney, the law library, the judge, the county commissioners, and the county clerk. The building has the reputation of having one of the grandest courtrooms in the state. DeLongchamps's plans specified a ceiling light and an interior richly appointed in wood. He allocated space for the jail in the basement. A large modern addition for city offices and the sheriff is attached to the courthouse to the rear, and it stands on the site of a jail that predated the construction of the 1919 DeLongchamps courthouse.

Beginning in 1949 DeLongchamps prepared a series of plans to alter the courthouse, but the county never initiated the project.[9] A 1976 passageway, connecting the old courthouse to the new county office building to the rear, has a minimal effect on the original courthouse.[10] Instead the grand building remains as a monumental symbol of one of the oldest counties of the state.

10 : LANDER COUNTY

Lander County officials have been housed in three structures, each built in a different county seat. All three buildings represent an important bench mark in the history of courthouse architecture in Nevada. The courthouse in Jacobsville was the first constructed in the territory. The second, erected in Austin, is the clearest expression of Greek Revival courthouse architecture in the state. The third, a structure in Battle Mountain, is a recent, imaginative adaptation of a historic school.

The territorial legislature created Lander County on December 19, 1862, and it was the first formed after the designation of the original nine in 1861. Lander County was carved out of the northeast corner of the territory from Humboldt and Churchill Counties. At the time of its creation, it represented about one-third of Nevada's land. It subsequently yielded territory to additional counties and is now the ninth largest county in Nevada with 5,621 square miles. The rush to the Reese River Mining District, which inspired the creation of the county, nevertheless, proved less dynamic than many hoped, and it left the recently developed region sparsely populated. Initially, the commissioners met in Jacobsville—also known as Jacob's Springs—where they evidently could not find a suitable structure to serve as a courthouse. Consequently on April 29, 1863, they paid J. A. McDonald $8,440 to build a simple wooden courthouse. The single-story structure measured 20 x 40 feet. It was clad in 1-inch clapboard and rose to a plain-box cornice and shingled roof. A porch spanned the width of the front, supported by plain 2 x 4-inch columns. Windows on the side elevations provided natural light for the courtroom, and the interior featured a balustrade that separated the proceedings from the audience. The judge's bench was elevated by an 18-inch platform from which to dispense justice.[1]

A few months after McDonald completed the building, the effects of a new mineral strike necessitated change. The discovery of silver ore drew hundreds to the new community of Austin, which soon overshadowed the tiny settlement of Jacobsville. The Lander County commissioners transferred the seat of government to Austin with apparently little or no opposition. They then paid McDonald to move his small, undistinguished structure and to construct a stone basement at its new location.

McDonald was almost certainly not a trained architect. He was probably a local builder, familiar with the techniques necessary to erect a structure that would not easily fall down. Apparently the people of Austin regarded McDonald's building as temporary, and they soon afterwards sought the construction of a monumental courthouse. They knew all too well how easily shifts in population, power, and government could occur. The lesson to be learned from the previous move of government was to build in brick. A heavy and substantial structure would do its part to discourage another community from taking the seat of government. County commissioners began plans for a new facility. By the time the original frame structure had stood for only eight years, a county newspaper proclaimed that "she is now old, and will soon be discarded to give way to the elegant and substantial building now in progress of erection."[2]

On September 9, 1871, dignitaries laid the cornerstone for the new courthouse in Austin, which included such memorabilia as the proceedings of the ceremony, four stereoscopic photo-

Lander County completed its courthouse in Austin in 1872. Although the county seat has since moved to Battle Mountain, this structure still houses county offices. (Nevada Historical Society)

graphs of the city, a bar of Reese River silver bullion, American and Chinese coins, a piece of ore, and copies of the *Reese River Reveille* and *Drych*—a Welsh newspaper.[3] Designed by Dan P. Bell and built by contractors Bliss and Mahoney, it is Nevada's only remaining Greek Revival courthouse. Many individuals once considered this type of architecture as the perfect expression of democratic ideals, but by the time of the building of the Lander County Courthouse, the style had ceased to be fashionable. The *Reese River Reveille* said that it was in "the ionian [sic] style of architecture." The paper continued to say that "we will hope . . . that the record of crime to be

This nineteenth-century photograph shows Judge Malloy in the county clerk's office in the Lander County Courthouse. Note the elaborate wallpaper and tin ceiling. (Nevada Historical Society)

tried within the walls of the new Court house may go on diminishing as civilization advances."[4] The building cost about $30,000, including furniture and adjacent lots—not an exorbitant price to pay for civilization.

Work progressed rapidly on the courthouse, which builders finished on January 17, 1872. The structure remains as an imposing presence on Austin's Main Street. A substantial stone foundation supports the 44 x 62-foot two-story brick courthouse. A gabled roof rests on a front pediment with a brick dentil cornice, all in the Greek Revival style, and an oculus, or a round window, graces the pediment. The symmetrical five-bay façade includes a double-door with transom—a window above the entrance. The second-floor door on the front elevation opens to an iron balcony. As in most courthouses of the period, the courtroom is on the second floor together with a jury room and the judge's chambers. In addition, the top floor housed the county clerk. The first floor included other county offices and four jail cells. Adopting typical rhetoric for the opening of a courthouse, the *Reese River Reveille* commented: "We do not believe that there was ever erected in this state a public building of that size and quality for anything like that amount of money. The building is an ornament to the city."[5] This was probably a fair assessment. The unpretentious courthouse is sturdy and substantial with an uncluttered simplicity that gives it one of the most impressive façades in the state. Oddly, the obituary for Bell, its architect, makes no mention of the courthouse but merely states: "He was a splendid mechanic, as a dozen quartz mills put up by him throughout California, Nevada and Utah will show."[6] His friends appear to have remembered him more for his industrial designs than this important structure. Bell committed suicide in July 1877 after attempts to cure a cancer of the face failed.

Even though the original courthouse held an important position as the first such structure built in Nevada, the old wooden facility, which survived the move from Jacobsville to Austin and served the county for nearly ten years, was sold for lumber. There had been talk of moving the hospital into the building, but locals complained that the "rickety old courthouse frame is like a bake oven in the warm season and a refrigerator in winter."[7] County leaders concluded that the lumber would be better used for new construction. Other portions of the courthouse, including the foundation, may have been used but their ultimate fate is unknown.

Spanning the decades, Lander County endured repeated attempts to move the seat of government from Austin to Battle Mountain in the north. The region's mining district declined in the late nineteenth century, leaving behind a local economy based on county government and transportation. The Lincoln Highway, the first transcontinental road, passed through Austin in the 1920s. Nevertheless, with the opening of U.S. Route 40 and Interstate 80 to the north and the development of mining districts in northern Nevada later in the twentieth century, Battle Mountain grew to rival Austin. Still, the old community used repeated, imaginative maneuvers to block several attempts in the twentieth century for a county-seat shift.[8]

Finally, in May 1979 Battle Mountain succeeded by popular vote in securing the seat of government, which transferred north. Shortly after the shift, Lander County officials authorized work on a former school in Battle Mountain.[9] The remodeled 1916 structure has the same ceremonial trappings of other Neo-Classical courthouses in Nevada. With sensitive rehabilitation, county officials avoided the cost of new construction and obtained a grand courthouse designed in the historical tradition of the state. The rehabilitation of the historic structure is a good expression of the most recent period of courthouse construction, dominated as it was by pragmatism and economic concerns. The occupation of the old schools, however, provided a shortcut to monumental architecture construction and furnished Lander County officials with a facility that compared nicely with those of the rest of the state (see the photographs in chapter 19). The 1871 Greek Revival courthouse continues to serve as a regional county office building.

The three courthouses of Lander County testify to the nature of the remote, thinly populated region. The first two courthouses were constructed in Jacobsville and Austin because no other temporary facility was available in the tiny young communities. Circumstance forced the commissioners to go through considerable effort to erect a facility at a time when many other counties sought to rent or otherwise obtain temporary accommodations. The Austin courthouse is a fine expression of Greek Revival architecture, but it was constructed nearly a dozen years after most architects in the nation had abandoned the style.[10] The late occurrence of the Greek Revival design in Nevada serves as evidence of the remoteness of the nineteenth-century American West, and its appearance in Austin underscores the isolation of that community in the state. The adaptive reuse of a historic structure in late-twentieth-century Battle Mountain reflects the relative lack of a tax base as the commissioners sought alternatives to expensive new construction.

11 : LINCOLN COUNTY

In 1872 Lincoln County officials moved into their new facility in Pioche that soon became the object of scorn and ridicule, eventually being referred to in Nevada folklore as the "Million Dollar Courthouse." It was constructed about the same time that Lander County erected its second courthouse. Unlike the Greek Revival structure of Austin, however, the Lincoln County Courthouse exhibited the more contemporary Italianate style. Although in a remote area of Nevada, Pioche served as an important hub of activity, and its public-works projects attracted experienced design expertise. Nevertheless, it has been famous for the county's inept financing of the courthouse that resulted in a debt reaching nearly seven figures. As a fitting commentary on how badly the county handled the situation, officials retired the structure, which was in serious need of repair, in the 1930s just as they finished payment on its bond issue. Although the building still stands, the county replaced it with a modest facility that is significant because it is the only Art Deco county courthouse in Nevada.

Lincoln County, created on February 25, 1866, honors the president whose assassination at the time was still a fresh memory in the minds of Americans. The county seat was initially located at Crystal Springs, but the government soon moved to Hiko. After months of delay, the county commissioners leased Butler's and Pearson's saloon for use as a courthouse. They later transferred their offices across the street to another building. It appears that the county never constructed a permanent courthouse until the seat of government moved in 1871 to Pioche, a booming mining town.[1]

Shortly after their move to Pioche, the county commissioners rushed into courthouse construction. They acquired a site that was separate from the chief business district and proceeded with the architectural plan designed by T. Dimmock and Thomas Keefe for a substantial 40 x 60-foot brick building. On August 28, 1871, the county awarded a construction contract of $16,400 to Edward Donahue.[2] John A. Steele designed a separate 20 x 30-foot two-story jail to the rear of the courthouse at a projected cost of $10,000. Steele was probably the same person who built the Washoe County Courthouse in Washoe City. He came to Pioche during its boom period and set up a contracting business with a local merchant, offering "plans and specifications for all kinds of buildings."[3]

Initially, the county issued a comprehensive contract for the construction of the courthouse, but within a short time changes to the building design and the corresponding financing increased the cost. The county finally broke the contract and awarded the work on a piecemeal basis, at higher prices. By the time the courthouse and jail were completed on March 16, 1872, the cost had risen to $75,000.

Over the years that followed, interest on the courthouse debt mounted making it even more unmanageable. When the county finally retired the debt in 1938, no one could be certain

The first Lincoln County Courthouse in Pioche dates to 1872. (Kathryn M. Kuranda)

exactly how much the building had cost. Local people were probably not far from the figure when they called it the "Million Dollar Courthouse." In his monograph on Lincoln County, James W. Hulse estimated that the total reached $800,000.[4]

In spite of the problems surrounding it, the building remains as a substantial presence in Pioche. Its simple Italianate design includes plain pilasters, a second-story balcony, and a fanlight above the front entrance. The structure has a brick front elevation with rubble side walls. Its elegant courtroom on the second floor is 40 x 30 feet. In 1873, shortly after the completion of the courthouse, the *Pioche Record* reported: "The building presents a good external appearance, and the sight of such an imposing edifice is calculated to give the traveller a good impression of our county and town."[5] There is little doubt that the courthouse was intended to present an image of law and order. The mining boomtown had developed a reputation for just the opposite, reinforced by a multitude of violent deaths in the early development of the community. Ironically, the impressive brick façade did little, in the long run, to improve the perception of Pioche. In fact, it eventually gave the county a reputation for fiscal mismanagement. Problems associated with the financing of the Lincoln County Courthouse notwithstanding, the structure is an unpretentious example of the elegant architecture of the period.

Still, the building also serves as a reminder that courthouse construction alone is insufficient to produce a good image for a county. No amount of architectural style can compensate for poor management in a public office. Even after the construction of the courthouse, continuing financial troubles further damaged the reputation of Lincoln County. Lack of funds to maintain prisoners adequately prompted the *Pioche Record* in 1876 to suggest a tongue-in-cheek solution:

The best action the officers can take in the premises . . . is to take the offender immediately to the County Jail, lock him up and take no more notice of him. If he digs his way out, all right, if he dies, it will not be much loss to the community, and if his friends can feed him so much the better for the prisoner.[6]

The entrance to the 1872 Lincoln County Courthouse shows a simple, tasteful use of nineteenth-century architectural details. (Kathryn M. Kuranda)

The county ignored this unorthodox advice, and two months later Lincoln County officials had to release an accused murderer because friends of the victim refused to continue paying for the prisoner's board. The local newspaper objected to such a practice and maintained that "the people of Pioche now seem to have no security for their lives or property, although they are heavily burdened with taxes."[7] The courthouse was far from being a universal panacea for the community.

In fact, the original Lincoln County Courthouse in Pioche had structural problems almost from the start. Adding insult to the financial injury that the building represented, major faults in the structure began to appear as early as 1879. At the same time, portions of the ceiling collapsed. Other problems continued to plague the county until officials decided a replacement was in order.[8]

With the anticipated retirement of the courthouse bonds in 1938, it was financially possible to consider a new structure. In addition, in 1937 Pioche started two decades of lead-zinc production, helping to give the county a better economic base. The local boom made Pioche an anomaly during the Great Depression and, indeed, during the mid-twentieth century. It was the only Nevada county to build a courthouse between 1922 and 1958.

The county commission accepted plans for the building on September 7, 1937, from Las Vegas architect A. Lacy Worswick. It subsequently awarded a construction contract to L. F. Dow of Los Angeles and Las Vegas. The structure, accepted by the Lincoln County commission on December 17, 1938, represents an important transition in the evolution of public architecture in Nevada. It is, above all, functional and places little stress on its ceremonial role. Its plain application of Art Deco design emphasizes financial considerations. Art Deco celebrated America's twentieth-century fascination with technology through its stylized ornamentation and structural mass. The Lincoln County Courthouse thus promoted an image of being in step with the rest of the nation and its technological revolution. Art Deco eventually ceased to be fashionable, but not before establishing a precedent for the emphasis of structural forms over ornamentation. The courthouse in Pioche marks this transition in the development of Nevada's county buildings.

The Lincoln County Courthouse is also notable for its modest size and cost. Its predecessor had become a symbol of fiscal mismanagement, and it took the county almost seventy years to settle the debt. When contemplating a new courthouse, Lincoln County officials naturally

The Lincoln County Courthouse built in 1938 is the only Art Deco courthouse in the state. (Kathryn M. Kuranda)

strived to avoid another financial blunder. They paid Dow Construction $50,000 for the struc-
ture, a debt that was retired in less than twenty years.[9]

The limited budget for the Lincoln County Courthouse resulted in a simple building with
efficient use of space. The white-concrete two-story structure has a flat roof and modest ornamentation. In contrast with earlier courthouses, much of this building lacks monumental or
public proportions. Although the courtroom has a grand scale similar to that of earlier courthouses, the remainder of the structure is largely functional.

Worswick, the architect, is responsible for many other important buildings in southern
Nevada and played a part in the development of Las Vegas during its boom period of the 1930s
and 1940s. He designed the Las Vegas Hospital (destroyed by fire in 1988), the Apache Hotel at
Second and Fremont Streets, and numerous houses, local movie theaters, grocery stores, service
stations, and office buildings. Worswick probably came to Las Vegas in 1929. He was a native of
Kansas and a graduate of Kansas State University. He began his architectural career in San
Francisco in 1902, and two years later he joined the city's Bureau of Architecture. As with
DeLongchamps, it appears that Worswick had a role in the rebuilding of San Francisco after the
1906 earthquake and fire. His career continued in Las Vegas into the 1940s, leaving a remarkable
assemblage of structures.[10] His building in Pioche provides an important link between two eras of
county courthouse construction in Nevada. Appropriately, he selected a style and approach that
looked to the future rather than referred to the past.

12 : LYON COUNTY

Lyon County has built two courthouses, each representing an architectural vanguard in the state. The territorial legislature created Lyon County on November 25, 1861. Situated on the eastern slope of the Sierra Nevada, the county included communities established in the 1850s. Although it remained largely rural, Lyon County's proximity to Virginia City, Carson City, and Reno meant that it participated in much of the region's economic success. This in turn was apparent by county officials' willingness to invest funds in public architecture from the start.

Dayton, a milling town on the Carson River, became Lyon County's first seat of government. After occupying temporary structures there for two years, Lyon County officials decided that a permanent, more impressive facility was in order. They subsequently commissioned one of the earliest courthouses in the state (only those of Lander and Washoe Counties predate it), and it was completed in the fall of 1864. Henry Sweetapple supervised the construction of the understated vernacular courthouse with Italianate details. Despite its simplicity, the building was clearly important for the area. The *Gold Hill Daily News*, for example, maintained that "The County Court House, just completed, is altogether the finest building of its kind in the State."[1] In 1864 this statement was not saying a great deal. Nevadans had not been in the business of building monumental architecture for long, and yet the courthouse set the tone for the young

The 1864 Lyon County Courthouse in Dayton was a sturdy brick structure that was destroyed by fire in 1909. (Nevada Historical Society)

state. It was, after all, a substantial building intended to last. The two-story brick building had an elaborate, molded cornice and well-defined brick corner pilasters. It had six jail cells made of solid masonry on the main floor and ample room for offices throughout. It is unclear exactly how much the structure cost, but the state legislature set an upper limit of $30,000 for the bonding capacity of the project.[2] Shortly after the Lyon County Courthouse opened, the Dayton Guard held a grand ball in the building. It was a momentous occasion for the community, and many must have regarded the building as a grand gift for a state less than a month old.

Perhaps the Lyon County Courthouse was most notable because of its Italianate architectural design. While counties in Nevada before and after employed the outdated Greek Revival style for public facilities, the building in Dayton was in step with national trends. In spite of the architectural bench mark the courthouse represented, it nevertheless attracted some early criticism. Before construction proceeded, the local *Como Sentinel* commented that the building site was selected in such a way that "on a windy day, with proper attention to ventilation, any amount of dust can be obtained with little expense."[3] Still, when fire destroyed the courthouse on May 15, 1909, many in Dayton felt it as a great loss.

Soon after the fire, the citizens of Yerington to the south circulated a petition calling for the shift of the county seat to their community. A lengthy and heated political battle ensued. In March 1910 Lyon County commissioners authorized contractor George King to begin reconstruction of the Dayton facility in spite of the political turmoil. Nearly a year later, in January 1911, the Nevada State Legislature resolved the controversy by shifting the seat of government to Yerington and consequently made the work at Dayton useless. The change echoed the region's transformation from a predominant reliance on mining—Dayton originally served as a mill town—to farming. Yerington's proximity to the Sierra Nevada range afforded it access to sufficient water for irrigating lush fields, and, as a result, its agriculture provided a stable economic foundation.

Although Dayton claimed that the county-seat move violated the state constitution, a district court upheld the legislative action, and the plans for the construction of the present Lyon County Courthouse proceeded. On April 12, 1911, the county commissioners accepted De-Longchamps's designs. Located on Main and Grove Streets on land donated by Mary Burton, the building became the second courthouse of the Nevada architect's distinguished career. DeLongchamps applied Beaux-Arts architecture less strictly than he had in his earlier Washoe County Courthouse, beginning a trend towards a more subtle Neo-Classical design.

The budget allocated $35,000 for the construction of the courthouse, $3,000 for a separate jail, and $4,000 for the interior furnishings. Ward Brothers and Calder of Reno were the building contractors, and George W. Hollsworth served as the superintendent of construction. In November 1911 the county amended the courthouse architectural program to integrate a jail. By December work had progressed sufficiently for the commissioners to award contracts for the interior furnishings. Although the *Mason Valley News* voiced concern over the quality of construction as early as June 1911, the county commissioners did not address the issue until late December when the southern section of the building collapsed. The damage was so severe that future Nevada governor James G. Scrugham, then Nevada State Engineer, launched an investigation. The contractors initially suggested that vandals had used dynamite to destroy the building. Later investigation results of the incident implied that DeLongchamps's plans were inferior and caused the disaster. Nevertheless, a formal inquiry found DeLongchamps blameless and cited the construction company as responsible for faulty cement work.

After undergoing repairs, the Lyon County Courthouse opened its doors in the spring of 1912. The brick structure has many Beaux-Arts features and also integrates a late nineteenth-century eclectic style of ornamentation, including a highly sculpted cornice with dentils. Both sides of the granite entrance steps are decorated with ornamental iron lamp posts that have glass globes. A concrete waterline caps a stone foundation, and frames for the front double doors and windows include pedimented ornamentation. Four-paired terra cotta columns support a massive porch with a large pediment that establishes the principal elevation as an ornamental adaptation of classical motifs. DeLongchamps's plans called for a tin-standing seam roof with galvanized iron trim.

Like the majority of DeLongchamps's courthouse designs, the building includes a central hall with flanking offices. The hall has a floor made of small tiles reminiscent of those of the Washoe County Courthouse in Reno, which had been designed two years before by DeLongchamps. The Lyon County Courthouse differed from its predecessor, however, in the use of large

DeLongchamps designed the Lyon County Courthouse in Yerington, which was completed in 1912 and still serves the county. (Ronald M. James)

white and green tile squares that formed a 6-foot-high wainscotting for all interior halls. The first floor of the structure included space for the assessor, sheriff, auditor, and recorder. Opposite the sheriff's office was a jail designed to accommodate twelve prisoners. Today, you can still see the massive, central open stairway, with an oak balustrade, which provides access to the second story. The doors to the courtroom stand at the head of the staircase, and inside are well-preserved expressions of period design including finish work in oak details. Opposite the courtroom is office space for the judge, the clerk, treasurer, and district attorney as well as for a stenographer and reporters.[4] DeLongchamps's plans also called for a third-story jury room and space in the basement for a vault.

With the traditional boosterism inspired by the opening of a courthouse, the *Yerington Times* commented that "Lyon County has the largest, best built, best furnished and best looking courthouse in the state for the money. Every taxpayer in the county should feel proud of such a building."[5] Like the earlier courthouse in Dayton, the Yerington building was one of the first monumental expressions of the period's architecture in the state.

In 1935 DeLongchamps designed an addition for the rear of the courthouse. Made of brick with windows of similar proportions, the addition is virtually indistinguishable from the remainder of the building, except for its lacking extensive window ornamentation.[6] The county recently constructed an additional structure to the rear of the courthouse. Echoing the dentil cornice and other details of its older neighbor, the newer brick building is compatible with the larger courthouse. In spite of the two additions to the complex, the courthouse remains in a spacious, parklike setting with mature trees, which provides the community with its most significant green space on Main Street.

13 : MINERAL COUNTY

Mineral County has an unusual courthouse history, since it has the only courthouse in Nevada to have served two county governments. Hawthorne was the Esmeralda County seat from 1883 until 1907, at which time county officials moved south to Goldfield. When the state legislature created Mineral County in 1911, the Hawthorne courthouse once again served as the seat of government. The county only recently replaced the building with one of the newest courthouses in the state.

Hawthorne's courthouse was constructed in 1883 and remains as one of the most monumental structures in the community. Esmeralda County commissioners originally developed building specifications for a wooden-frame courthouse, but after a brick yard opened nearby for the McKenzieville reduction plant, the county agreed to use the more durable material.[1] They appointed A. C. Glenn as supervising architect and gave George W. Babcock a construction contract for $29,125. The plans were for a 36 x 64-foot building with 14-foot-high ceilings on each floor. The courtroom was designed to be 30 x 36 feet with a monumental 16-foot-high ceiling.[2] Groundbreaking ceremonies occurred on August 16, 1883, and officials laid the cornerstone one month later on September 8. The county had its new courthouse ready on December 5, 1883, but not before numerous changes to the contract had escalated the cost to $33,967. During construction, the county dismissed Glenn from the project for reasons unclear in the

The courtroom of the monumental Mineral County Courthouse, completed in 1883, eventually received criticism for being too small. (Photo ca. 1890; courtesy of the Nevada Historical Society)

historical record. D. R. Munro replaced him and completed the building. An 1884 Esmeralda County grand jury investigated the problems with the project and found that the structure was substantially different from the authorized plans. It criticized county officials, stating that there were: "a great many changes in said building, which, with but one exception, were to the advantage of the contractor, and in no way advantageous to the county."[3] In spite of the local controversy, the Esmeralda County Courthouse became a significant statement of Hawthorne's prosperity and permanence. Like other courthouses constructed in Nevada at the time, this building was meant to last and to be impressive. It succeeded on this level in spite of concerns about the soundness of its construction.

The courthouse is a two-story Italianate building with buttressed sidewalls supported by a raised basement. Slightly arched brick window and door openings are devoid of decoration. Central gables accent the courthouse's four elevations, and a bracketed cornice bands the roof line. The structure has an unusual five-sided, semicircular entry porch with wooden columns and a pentagram-design balustrade. The National Emergency Recovery Act project in the 1930s altered the building with the construction of a concrete vault to the rear. In addition, county officials removed the cupola, which originally graced the structure's roof, because it was apparently too heavy.[4] Nevertheless, the courthouse, which stands on a landscaped site with mature trees, still retains much of its original design.[5]

Shortly after the turn of the century, the mining boom at Tonopah and Goldfield inspired a rush to the southern part of the county. Goldfield quickly became the largest community in the state. Far removed from Hawthorne, the citizens of Goldfield soon began to call for a county-seat shift. The subsequent move of the county government to Goldfield, in 1907, occurred in the face of bitter opposition from the citizens of Hawthorne (see chapter 7). In fact, they remained hostile over the county-seat move for years afterwards, and a nearby mining boom in 1908 seemed to vindicate those who said that the change to Goldfield was premature. Citizens from the northern end of Esmeralda County approached the state legislature in 1911 and requested that the county be divided. Although there was initial opposition from some legislators, a bill eventually passed, authorizing the creation of Mineral County with Hawthorne as its seat. The new government established offices in the former Esmeralda County Courthouse in Hawthorne, making this 1883 building the only structure in Nevada to have served as a public facility for two counties. It was condemned in 1974, but the courthouse remains a monumental, though uninhabited, presence in the community.

The first Mineral County Courthouse in Hawthorne also served Esmeralda County. The Italianate building still stands but is no longer used. (Photo ca. 1883; Nevada Historical Society)

In the late 1960s Mineral County commissioners began considering the erection of a new courthouse. District Judge Kenneth L. Mann argued that this was needed when he stated that

> A courtroom is many things. It is a place where all of our citizens have equal access to a court of law. It is a place where juries, attorneys, the court officials and the judge serve the people of this county, attempting to disperse equal justice to all in each case.[6]

The judge argued that the 1883 courtroom did not have sufficient space to handle the judicial process because it did not provide the public proper access. After deliberating on the problem,

The second Mineral County Courthouse, completed in 1970, includes references to classical architectural motifs. (Kathryn M. Kuranda)

Mineral County commissioners decided to proceed with the new construction. Using the plans of Lockard and Casazza of Reno, on August 6, 1969, the county awarded the building contract to A. S. Johnson Construction Company of Sparks for $331,629. Work began immediately and officials dedicated the cornerstone on September 13. The courthouse was completed later the next year. It is a sprawling, 9,000-square-foot, single-story brick structure with a flat roof. A dentil cornice and stylized columns lend a classical air to the functional structure.[7] The building diverges from the traditional symmetrical floor plan of earlier courthouses. The ceremonial entrance, signified by four square-brick columns provides access to a corner of the building. Inside, a lobby opens to the county administrative offices and a hallway. A turn of the central corridor leads to the courtroom and related judicial facilities. Function rather than need for ceremonial balance determines the arrangement of space.[8] Mineral County officials subsequently constructed the Public Safety Building to house the district attorney, the sheriff, and the jail separate from the other county offices.

14 : NYE COUNTY

Nye County has erected two courthouses, each of which exhibits current tastes in architectural design. The first, built in Belmont, is one of the most distinctive expressions of Italianate architecture in Nevada. The second is the courthouse built in turn-of-the-century Tonopah. It is the only county facility in the state with Romanesque Revival details.

Nye County commissioners approached courthouse construction methodically during the nineteenth century, unlike many others in Nevada's mining regions. The legislature named the county after James Warren Nye, governor of the Nevada Territory and subsequently U.S. senator from the new state. Officials did not organize their government until 1864, positioning their first seat at Ione.[1] Although the county commission allocated $800 for the building of a courthouse, it appears that officials never undertook the task. Whether spent or not, the low funding was prudent. As Angel suggests about Nye County: "There was not that unbridled extravagance in the management of its financial affairs which characterized and distinguished many of the county organizations of the State."[2] The Nevada State Legislature moved the county seat in February 1867 from Ione, with its failing mining economy, to Belmont, a young boomtown. The county conducted its business in several buildings for the next eight years.[3] It was not until the mid-1870s that Nye County began pursuing the erection of a monumental courthouse. Perhaps the area's remoteness and sparse population left the residents of Belmont without the threat of a county-seat move and uninterested in a hasty expenditure of public funds.

In 1875 Nye County commissioners reviewed seven courthouse design proposals and accepted J. K. Winchell's plans for a new two-story brick building.[4] Winchell was an architect in Carson and Virginia Cities and had a few months before designed the grounds and fence for the Nevada State Capitol.[5] In August 1875 the Nye County commission awarded the construction contract for $22,000 for its courthouse to J. T. Benham of Reno. The *Territorial Enterprise* suggested that the building "will be of a modern style of architecture, and will present an imposing appearance." It went on to say: "Connected with it, in the rear, will be the jail."[6] Stonemasons quarried nearby granite for the foundation, and workers made the brick at the construction site. The square Italianate Belmont courthouse had corner pilasters, a simple bracketed cornice, six brick chimneys, and a Tuscan cupola.[7] On July 4, 1876, the nation's centennial, the citizens of Nye County held an Independence Day ball, the first function in the new courthouse.

At the turn of the century a major mineral strike to the south and west of Belmont initiated the state's twentieth-century mining boom. The town of Tonopah, founded on the Nye-Esmeralda county border, sprung to life with an explosiveness rivaling any nineteenth-century boomtown. By 1905 its dramatic growth, combined with the profound depression of the mining industry in the area of Belmont, prompted the state legislature to move the county offices to the newer, more prosperous community.[8] Deprived of the county government, its last industry, Belmont continued to dwindle. On August 20, 1974, ownership of the old Belmont courthouse transferred to the Nevada state government. Managed by the Division of State Parks, the dilapidated structure underwent an extensive rehabilitation that saved it from becoming a standing ruin.

Tonopah quickly broke with the plodding construction practice that Belmont established

The former Nye County Courthouse in Belmont served the county from 1875 to 1905, when the seat of government moved to Tonopah; today the Nevada Division of State Parks manages the structure. (Photo ca. 1880; courtesy of the Nevada Historical Society)

during the previous century and rushed into building its courthouse. As the *Tonopah Sun* reported in April 1905: "The courthouse and county jail are to be built in Tonopah as fast as material can be obtained and men perform the task."[9] The commissioners awarded the Continental Construction Company a contract for $28,000. "The building will be an ornament to the camp," continued the *Tonopah Sun*. The *Tonopah Bonanza* added: "The plans for the building, which will be a pretentious affair, were drawn by J. C. Robertson, one of the best architects on the Pacific coast."[10] Despite some pressure to place the courthouse in the commercial center of town,

The 1905 Nye County Courthouse in Tonopah has a dome and Romanesque arches. (Photo ca. 1910; courtesy of the Nevada Historical Society)

The courtroom of the turn-of-the-century courthouse in Tonopah showed formal finish work. Arrangements for lighting, however, were not as elegant. (Photo ca. 1910; courtesy of the Nevada Historical Society)

the county selected a site on the Gold Hill land donated by the Tonopah Mining Company. By June 1905 the county laid the cornerstone for its new courthouse.[11]

The two-story coursed ashlar stone, concrete building was completed within the year, under the direction of E. E. Burdick, a local artisan. The courthouse, originally measuring 50 x 60 feet, has a moderately pitched pyramidal roof and is crowned by a dome and eaves that include a classical, molded cornice dressed with dentils. Clustered columns support round arches making this the only county courthouse in Nevada with substantial Romanesque elements. Robertson designed the first floor to provide space for the assessor, sheriff, county commissioners, clerk, treasurer, auditor, and recorder. A central hallway leading directly from the front door provides access to offices. The courtroom and the offices of the district attorney and the judge are located on the second floor, which is roughly 29 x 47 feet. To the rear of these offices was an area for the jury, including a large-jury dormitory. A two-tier *jail tank* occupied the rear of the building.[12]

Robertson designed a two-story jail addition to the structure in 1907. Its coursed ashlar stone matches the original structure. Much later in the 1960s three additions included wings to the sides and to the rear of the structure. They were built of concrete block with vertically grouped windows and a flat roof. Recently the county added a steel and glass porch to the entrance of the facility in Tonopah. These recent alterations detract from the architecture of this remarkable Romanesque Revival courthouse, but it nevertheless retains much of its original fabric.

15 : PERSHING COUNTY

The Pershing County Courthouse is round with Neo-Classical details that are well applied, although not remarkable, and built for $99,138.68—modest even for the 1920s.[1] Its size, at almost 16,000 square feet, makes it neither impressively large nor small. Instead, the courthouse deserves note for only one reason: its shape. With this simple distinctive feature, the Pershing County commissioners achieved what they wanted, a courthouse like none other in Nevada and perhaps in the nation.

Pershing County was originally part of Humboldt County. Shortly after the turn of the century, the people of Lovelock to the south began to complain that the county spent too much public funds in Winnemucca, the seat of government to the north. When the Humboldt County Courthouse burned in 1918, the residents in and near Lovelock insisted on dividing the county.

They felt that if their taxes were to support the construction of a new courthouse it should be for one in their own community, and they took their case to the state legislature. As a result, on March 18, 1919, governor Emmet D. Boyle signed legislation creating Nevada's seventeenth county, thus ending a dispute that had lasted for decades. The new county's name honors the popular general John J. "Blackjack" Pershing, leader of the American forces in World War I. The legislature designated Lovelock as the county seat.[2]

On March 27, 1919, the commissioners of the newly organized Pershing County established offices in the Lovelock Mercantile Building, but on September 5, 1919, they accepted an offer from the Pershing Hotel to relocate there for one year at $120 a month.[3] Impatient to house justice in more formal accommodations, the commissioners soon made plans for a courthouse. Lovelock was experiencing a building boom and many felt that the new growth should include a suitable courthouse to give public expression to the aspirations of the county. In addition, the rivalry with Humboldt County, their neighbor to the north, apparently motivated the community.[4]

While the Pershing County commissioners were organizing their new government, Humboldt County went forward with plans for a new courthouse in Winnemucca. To make sure that they had the best possible building, the Humboldt County commissioners solicited plans from DeLongchamps, who had already designed several other courthouses in Nevada. He was well known for his conservative monumental architecture, and his work must have seemed ideal for a community with deep historical roots as a commercial and governmental center.[5] DeLongchamps designed a large Neo-Classical courthouse that embodied the strength and stability of Humboldt County. At the same time, the Humboldt County commission launched a lawsuit to stop the organization of their new southern neighbor. But as a plaque on the wall of the Pershing County Courthouse states, a total eclipse on May 29, 1919, "should have been some sign to the Humboldt County officials as to the outcome of the lawsuit." In fact, the effort failed and Pershing County retained its independence.

Pershing County was neither to be extinguished nor outdone. Community leaders purchased almost two acres of open land at the end of the principal commercial axis of the community for their new public building.[6] Noted Reno architect George C. Ferris submitted a courthouse proposal to the commissioners in November 1919, but for whatever reason his plan was not used.[7] Instead, the commissioners turned to DeLongchamps for a courthouse design, but their needs differed from that of their northern neighbor. Lovelock was a younger community, and people perceived their town as progressive, booming, and destined to achieve a prominent place in northern Nevada. At the same time, their economy was based on agriculture, one of the most traditional endeavors. Pershing County needed an architect who would capture all of these facets in the design of their courthouse. DeLongchamps, a traditionalist by reputation, could clearly satisfy much of the community's needs for projecting the right persona, but mixing old images with new ones and being inventive at the same time would require finesse. In fact, there is a persistent local oral tradition that the county commissioners asked DeLongchamps to design something different from his previous works.[8] The result is one of his most distinctive buildings. The local *Review-Miner* stated that his design "will fit ideally with the proposed site."[9] It also suited local politics. After the county split, the natural rivalry between Lovelock and Winnemucca was heightened. Residents of Lovelock wanted their courthouse to outshine that of Humboldt County. It was a difficult goal because officials of the younger Pershing County had fewer economic resources than their mature neighbor to the north. What they could not acquire with grandiose spending, DeLongchamps achieved with imaginative design. The circle-over-hexagon plan that the architect proposed gave Pershing County the distinctive touch they wanted. On May 5, 1920, the county hired Howard S. Williams of San Francisco to build the

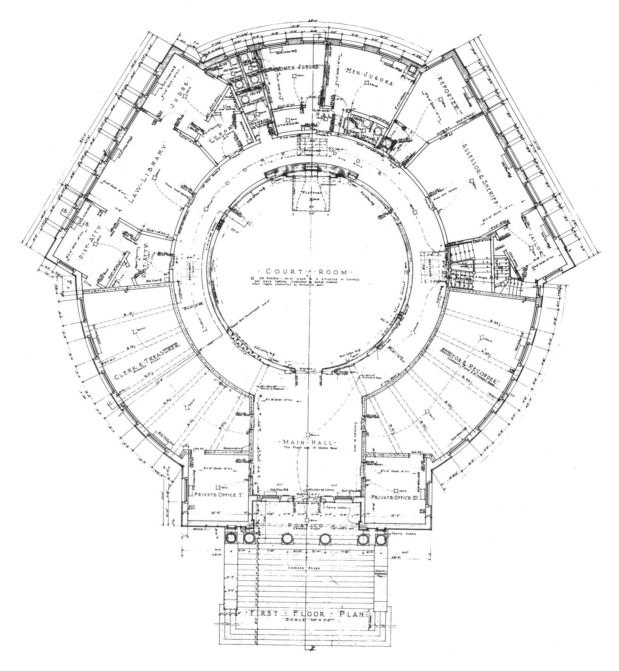

The main-floor ground plan of the Pershing County Courthouse illustrates the circle-over-hexagon design. The building is perhaps one of two round courthouses in the nation. (The DeLongchamps Collection, Getchell Library, University of Nevada, Reno)

courthouse. Jacob C. Meyer of Reno supplied the plumbing and heating. The estimated cost was almost $80,000, but by the time Lovelock celebrated its completion on June 20, 1921, the entire project had cost nearly $100,000.[10]

Like DeLongchamps's other public structures, the Pershing County Courthouse has traditional Neo-Classical elements. Six Ionic columns clad in terra cotta support a full-pedimented portico and define the building's entrance. Shallow Doric pilasters separate the main-story windows. The exterior of the building was finished in cream brick and terra cotta. The interior of the building includes a central circular courtroom that retains its original fixtures and canvas

The 1921 Neo-Classical Pershing County Courthouse was DeLongchamps's last design for a courthouse (additions aside) actually constructed in a Nevada county. (Ronald M. James)

The round courtroom of the Pershing County Courthouse lies in the center of the building. Its unique shape makes for a striking setting. (Ronald M. James)

ceiling. The acoustical design of the courtroom focuses the sound to the jury box in the center. Ornamental pilasters surmounted by a cartouche, accent the wall behind the judge's bench.[11] A hallway encircles the courtroom, giving access to county offices along the perimeter. The main floor housed the clerk, treasurer, auditor, recorder, district judge, district attorney, sheriff, assessor, and court reporter. In addition, DeLongchamps set aside room for the law library and jury. The basement included space for the justice of the peace, the county surveyor, the road supervisor, the county jail, and the heating plant. Throughout, Neo-Classical motifs dominated the structure.

With conventional details such as these, only its shape gives the courthouse a prominent place in architectural history. A nationwide survey turned up only one other example: The modern Bucks County Courthouse in Pennsylvania, constructed in 1960, is composed of round and rectangular sections.[12] The classical features of the Pershing County Courthouse bear the DeLongchamps imprint, but the device of making the courthouse round served to differentiate Pershing County from its northern neighbor. Like all the courthouses DeLongchamps designed, the Pershing County building demonstrated his academic background and his talent for giving people what they wanted.

DeLongchamps studied classical architecture and used it in designing the Pershing County courthouse. The round shape mimics the Roman Pantheon—the structure that inspired Thomas Jefferson in his design of the rotunda at the University of Virginia. This device was subsequently employed for the Jefferson Memorial, dedicated in 1943 in Washington, D.C.

The Pantheon was a temple to the gods of the Roman Empire. Christians later adapted it in their churches. When Jefferson selected it as his inspiration for the University of Virginia library, he made his position clear. Students were to study under the dome of the Rotunda, surrounded by books. His building sanctified learning, and knowledge was the cornerstone of Jefferson's university and nation. In the Pershing County Courthouse DeLongchamps sanctified justice, with the court occupying the holiest place—the center of the building.

The Pershing and Humboldt county commissions both wanted traditional and substantial courthouses to serve as symbols of permanence and stability. Pershing County's request for something different resulted in a unique building. Their courthouse is a sophisticated expression of architecture that simultaneously expresses the traditional aspirations of the community and the ambitious hopes of its people for the future. DeLongchamps demonstrated his talent by providing Pershing County with a courthouse that had a distinct classical design. This, his last Nevada courthouse, marks the end of a period of growth in public architecture that he began a dozen years before in Washoe County. The turn-of-the-century Beaux-Arts references of the Reno courthouse included a complicated adaptation of classical motifs that deviated in some ways from simpler prototypes. In his subsequent courthouses, DeLongchamps shed elaborate details and designed courthouses that progressively looked more like the elegant architecture of Greece and Rome. In Lovelock he completed his return to the classical world.[13]

In 1947 the Pershing County commission asked DeLongchamps to design an addition to the courthouse, but they never pursued construction of the rectangular wing. Instead, the unaltered monument remains as intended—in solitary grandeur, in the midst of an unspoiled park setting, and as a source of local pride.

16 : STOREY COUNTY

Storey County's courthouse is the most opulent of those built in nineteenth-century Nevada. Far exceeding the cost of its counterparts, the building served the state's richest community of the 1860s and 1870s. Ironically, the county built the courthouse at a time when Virginia City was about to collapse into near-permanent depression. Perhaps in partial recognition of this inevitable fate, local civic leaders rebuilt their town following the devastating fire of October 26, 1875, in a style grander than before. The Storey County Courthouse remains as a vivid example of this community's rebirth in the face of economic decline.

The fabulous wealth of the Comstock Lode made Storey County, established in 1861, famous throughout the world. In spite of the mining district's affluence, the county commission was reluctant to erect a formal courthouse. Indeed, they postponed the decision to do so for nearly fifteen years after the organization of the county. Public officials initially occupied the Odd Fellows Hall that stood on the site of the present courthouse. The simple, two-story structure was well suited for the county's immediate needs, but it still had problems typical of buildings adapted for public use. By the mid-1860s pressure mounted either to build a courthouse or to purchase a structure so that the county could cease paying rent.

In spite of the fact that the hall did little to project a sense of the region's wealth and prosperity, the commissioners chose to purchase and remodel it in 1865. They added, at considerable expense, two stories, a jail, and new vaults. This provided room for the growing county government and for the Odd Fellows and other secret associations, which took over the fourth floor.[1] Unfortunately, the weight of the new stories caused the courthouse to sway in strong winds, and in 1873 the commissioners spent more public funds to remove the top floor. Two years later, the great fire of 1875 destroyed the structure and forced the county to erect a new courthouse.

The construction project occurred surprisingly late, considering that Virginia City was the largest nineteenth-century community in Nevada. In fact, the need was probably greater than immediately apparent. Investors might have seen the failure to replace the courthouse with a substantial structure as an indication that the Comstock bonanza was drawing to a close. This is not directly evident given the fact that the mid-1870s was a time of fabulous productivity. Nevertheless, insiders knew that major miners had not located new, significant ore deposits and that the bullion produced represented the last of the famed big bonanza. The county commissioners placed their bet on success and made a clear declaration of their faith in the future by funding a sturdy building of grand design. Indeed, the swift action of the commission underscored the urgency of the situation. In less than two months, they secured plans and detailed specifications for the new courthouse from Kenitzer and Raun, a prominent San Francisco architectural firm.

Henry and Charles W. Kenitzer and Edward T. Raun made names for themselves through design work in California. Born in Saxony of the future Germany, Henry Kenitzer emigrated to the United States in 1854 before he turned thirty. His younger brother, Charles, followed in 1862. The Kenitzers, along with Raun who arrived in San Francisco in 1849, established a long-lived professional practice on the West Coast.[2] In deciding which of the firm's three proposals to accept, the county made it clear that it would spare no expense in its construction. Although the plan featuring a stone front was the cheapest, the commissioners selected the one that specified brick and iron. The third option, a brick and iron Gothic front, would have cost about the same. Their choice featured the latest in decorations and promised to enhance the reputation of the Comstock as a place of tremendous wealth. On June 25, 1876, the *Territorial Enterprise* proclaimed that it would "when completed, form one of the finest structures of the kind anywhere on the Pacific Coast."[3]

There was little need to select a courthouse site because the county retained ownership of the original lot. This meant, however, that in spite of the expense and attention given to its design, the courthouse would be removed from the main street by a block, and visitors would subsequently not rely on it to formulate an immediate impression of the city center.

The commissioners hired Peter Burke, a local contractor, to construct the building. Caleb Nutting and Son, of San Francisco, supplied the safes and built the jail. Although the contract secured the cost at $74,557.55, overruns and disputes led the county into protracted negotiations with Burke after the project's completion. The final cost of the courthouse eventually reached approximately $117,000.

Opened on February 17, 1877, the High Victorian Italianate building is the oldest structure

The 1877 courthouse in Virginia City (the cartouche says 1876) still serves Storey County and is one of the most elaborate period courthouses in Nevada. (Photo ca. 1880; courtesy of the Nevada Historical Society)

in Nevada still used as a courthouse. The elaborate ironwork decorating the façade was painted in contrasting colors to accentuate its details. The centennial date of *1876*, in large metal numbers and surrounded with ornate filigree and painted gold, accents the pedimented façade of the building.[4]

To finish the presentation, the commissioners purchased an unblindfolded statue of Lady Justice to grace a niche above the entrance. Andrew Fraiser, Storey County Commission Chairman, ordered the gold-painted statue from a catalog of the Seelig Fine Arts Foundation of Williamsburg, New York. Justice cost $236 including shipping.[5]

A set of the plans for the courthouse, received by the Storey County commissioners in June 1876, included an unblindfolded Justice that inspired commentary from the *Gold Hill Daily News*:

> The façade will be ornamented by a figure representing Justice, with scales and sword that are orthodoxically supposed to belong to her. In the drawing she is represented without her eyes being blindfolded, which may be objected to by some as unconventional, but when one considers that this representative dispenser of awards and punishments will be compelled to stand out and take all the sand thrown in her eyes by the Washoe zephyrs, it will be readily conceded that her eyesight would not last long enough for her to get so much as a glimpse of the great wealth to be obtained by wickedly swaying the scales of Right and Wrong. It makes but little difference whether the blind is on or off.[6]

The unblindfolded eyes of Virginia City's Lady Justice have attracted attention over the years, but perhaps more significant was the willingness of the commissioners to pay for the ornamentation. It is after all, the only exterior statue of Justice on a Nevada courthouse.

The fact that she lacks a blindfold was probably not, as is maintained in local lore, a commentary on frontier justice. Artisans have traditionally depicted the evenhanded Justice as a blindfolded maiden, but the use of the blindfold has not been universal. For the Greeks and Romans, Justice was a virgin with an unerring instinct for fairness. She did not need a blindfold. German artists of the sixteenth century had a different point of view. Appalled by the corruption of the courts, they satirized Justice as blindfolded and staggering around the courtroom. This may be the earliest manifestation of the blindfold.[7] Justice eventually shed the negative meaning of her blindfold, which became a standard part of her image. Still, some artists have rejected it.

Opposite:
Virginia City's statue of Lady
Justice is one of the few in the
nation without a blindfold.
(Ronald M. James)

A gas-light fixture in the 1877
Storey County Courthouse is
now outfitted with electricity.
(Ronald M. James)

After all, if Justice is truly just, she need not be blind. Although it is rare to see the piercing eyes of Justice, Virginia City's maiden does not stand alone. There are over twenty similar statues scattered from Benton County, Oregon, (1888–1889) to the Old Bailey in London, England,

(1907). As recently as 1973, W. C. "Brother Rat" Stanton sculpted a statue of Justice with eyes unveiled for the Madison County Courthouse in North Carolina.[8] In addition, the image of an unblindfolded Justice appears to have been surprisingly common. For example, the Grant Furni-

The sheriff's office in the Storey County Courthouse included a make-shift arrangement that extended gas from the ceiling to a desk lamp via a hose. (Nevada Historical Society)

ture Company of Gold Hill, Nevada, which provided much of the furnishings for the Storey County Courthouse, included such an image on its receipt.[9]

Apart from the issue of the blindfold, the large zinc statue can be interpreted to symbolize the wish to project an image of opulence at the time of the courthouse construction. Image making, as with the luxury of the building, did not stop with the exterior, however. Inside, expensive walnut, marble trim and finish work remains as a testimony to the county's wealth. An article in the *Territorial Enterprise*, celebrating the facility's opening, describes handsomely designed gas lamps and a large chandelier in the main entrance suspended from the 18-foot ceiling of the first floor. With pride typical of such an occasion, the newspaper added: "The

The Storey County jail was state of the art in 1877, when it first opened. (Photo ca. 1880; courtesy of the Nevada Historical Society)

courtroom is perhaps not excelled for beauty or finish or convenience of appointment by any similar room on the . . . coast, unless it be the one at San Jose."[10] Storey County officials did not wish to be outdone.

Not surprisingly, the complexity of the construction contract and the intricacies of local politics led to a lengthy court case to settle the bill. Long after the completion of the courthouse, there were accusations that the contractor, perhaps with county complacency, had used shortcuts to make excess profits from the project. In 1897, twenty years after the completion of the building, workmen discovered that its 26-inch exterior wall was hollow. Peter Burke, the contractor, had evidently swindled the county by not filling the brick dual-wall system with rubble as was customary. The *Territorial Enterprise* reported that locals recalled the incident involving William "Red Mike" Langan, a man who worked for Burke as a bricklayer on the courthouse. He was later arrested for murder and imprisoned in the facility he had helped build. Shortly after his incarceration, he escaped by digging through the wall, which he had apparently known to be hollow. The county subsequently went to great expense to line the cells with iron so that the incident would not be repeated.[11]

17 : WASHOE COUNTY

Reflecting the preeminence of Reno throughout much of Nevada history, the Washoe County Courthouse is one of the state's most monumental. It is also, however, the county's third structure, and the county was fifty years old before it built a facility with such architectural grandeur.

Washoe County was created in 1861 as one of the original nine counties of the territory. Washoe City, an ore milling, lumber, and agricultural center on the northwestern bank of Washoe Lake, was its premier community, and so it was the clear choice for the county seat. After organizing the government there, Washoe County commissioners moved from one commercial building to another for the first few months, in a vain attempt to secure adequate office space. Initially they occupied the Davis Building, then on February 18, 1862, they moved to the Rice and McLaughlin Building, which they rented for $525 a year. In July 1862, less than one year after the creation of the county, the commissioners advertised plans for a two-story brick or stone courthouse with a basement. It was to be the second erected in the territory.

In July 1863 they paid John A. Steele, a local builder, $40 for his courthouse plans. Steele did not use any single architectural style or fashion. His design pieced together elements of buildings that he must have previously seen. As a result, his plan called for strict symmetry, pedimented roof, and simple pilasters of Greek Revival architecture—a style in its final days of popularity during the 1860s. Its bracketed cornice and rounded arches were borrowed from the Italianate style. The building also had a second-story porch, a three-bay façade, and interior side chimneys.

Steele subsequently won the building contract, which allowed $15,000 for the courthouse and $3,740 for the jail. The Washoe Mill and Mining Company donated the land for the building. Completed before the end of 1863, its brick walls made it far more substantial than the first courthouse of Nevada—that of Lander County, which had been erected of wood only months earlier.[1]

By the mid-1860s silver mills along the Carson River assumed much of the mineral processing for the Comstock Mining District, leaving the Washoe City milling industry to wither. The local lumber and agricultural business did not promote growth, and so the community stagnated. Lake's Crossing to the north controlled the bridge across the Truckee and became a major mercantile center for distribution of supplies, again chiefly in support of the Comstock. Called Reno after 1868, the settlement also served the viable agricultural community in the Truckee Meadows. The railroad platted Reno and its presence meant that the community had direct access to the new transcontinental line. Clearly, Reno was destined to grow much larger than its southern neighbor.[2] In July 1868 Reno community leaders circulated a petition that called for a shift of the county seat. This, as with subsequent petitions, was unsuccessful, but time was on the side of Reno. After many local political maneuvers, the state legislature resolved the issue by authorizing the move in 1871. Although residents of Washoe City continued to question the legality of the action, the courts ultimately decided in favor of Reno, but not before considerable expense and the generation of ill will.[3]

Once the county settled the issue of its seat of government, controversy ensued over the selection of a site for a new courthouse. Myron C. Lake, a politically powerful Reno pioneer and owner of Lake's Crossing at the Truckee River, offered land south of the river. He also promised $1,500 to make his donation more attractive. The railroad, with its tracks laid parallel to the established commercial district, promoted Reno's growth in a lineal fashion along the north side of the river. Development to the south would have required continuous use of the river crossing to reach the majority of the community and the railroad. The proposed courthouse site, however, would have benefited Lake, who owned the toll bridge and property south of the river. Critics questioned the logic behind building a courthouse so far from Reno on the other side of the Truckee River. Nevertheless, the county accepted the gift and found itself in the midst of litigation, in which opponents attempted to stop the construction of the courthouse. The state supreme court eventually heard the case, dismissing it and thereby endorsing the county's site selection.[4]

In the fall of 1871 the county awarded Septimus F. Hoole a contract for $20,000 to build the courthouse. Hoole, a prominent member of the community, had already sold his courthouse plans to the county for $150. A veteran of the Mexican War, he became an active entrepreneur in northwestern Nevada. He submitted plans for several projects and eventually became owner of the Reno Planing Mill. After selecting Hoole, the county named James Z. Kelly as the supervising architect and construction began. Kelly, a well-known resident of Reno, was also responsible for directing several important building projects in northern Nevada. Besides his work on the Washoe County Courthouse, Kelly served as supervising architect for the Humboldt County Courthouse, which was erected one year later along much the same lines. He was a Freemason and served Washoe County as justice of the peace in 1870. He later moved to Tuscarora, in Elko County, where he founded a lodge of Freemasons and was eventually elected to the Nevada State Assembly.

The county laid the cornerstone for the building on June 22, 1872. According to Angel, the contents included:

> copies of the *Nevada State Journal*, the Reno *Crescent*, the Eureka *Sentinel*, the San Francisco *Chronicle*, and the Sacramento *Union*, pieces of United States currency, silver coins, copy of contract, speech of Hon. C. W. Kendell on artesian wells, and a number of other documents and articles.[5]

On January 24, 1873, Hoole completed the two-story brick Washoe County Courthouse. Later that year, the county commissioners sold the old courthouse in Washoe City for $250. The new owner demolished it for brick, which he sent to Carson City for use in the construction of a powder magazine.[6]

The Washoe County Courthouse in Reno was a modest Italianate brick structure with a second-story balcony above the main entrance, interior side chimneys, and a tin-covered, octagonal cupola, 10 feet in diameter and 16-feet tall, with windows. The courthouse was 58 x 79 feet and included five bays and granite steps on its front façade. A 12-foot-wide hall extended the depth of the building, and the lower floor included offices for the clerk, recorder, treasurer, sheriff, and jail. The upper floors also had room for offices and for a 35 x 58-foot courtroom, which included a gallery suspended above the entrance. As work progressed, the county altered the design plans, increasing the cost of the structure. Hoole filed suit against the county for what he felt was inadequate compensation for his work. The county eventually settled the claim, providing him with an additional $4,828. In the summer of 1879 the county added a fireproof vault and a large burglar-proof safe with a time lock to the courthouse. The Hall Safe and Lock Company installed them for $2,440.[7]

Washoe County commissioners began considering the replacement of the Reno courthouse before it was forty years old. Reno was functioning as a financial hub for the new mining boom in the state, and local leaders evidently decided it was time for a new, up-to-date image. In 1909 they announced a design competition that ultimately had a dramatic effect on the architectural history of the state. Among the competitors was a young DeLongchamps, who had recently

The second Washoe County Courthouse, constructed in Reno in 1873, was an Italianate structure with a cupola. (Photo ca. 1900; courtesy of the Nevada Historical Society)

returned from an apprenticeship with an architectural firm in San Francisco. DeLongchamps's plans for the Washoe County Courthouse won first prize in the competition and set his productive career in motion. His plan adapted a Neo-Classical design that was strongly influenced by the Beaux-Arts style. The decision to accept DeLongchamps's design was a clear indication of

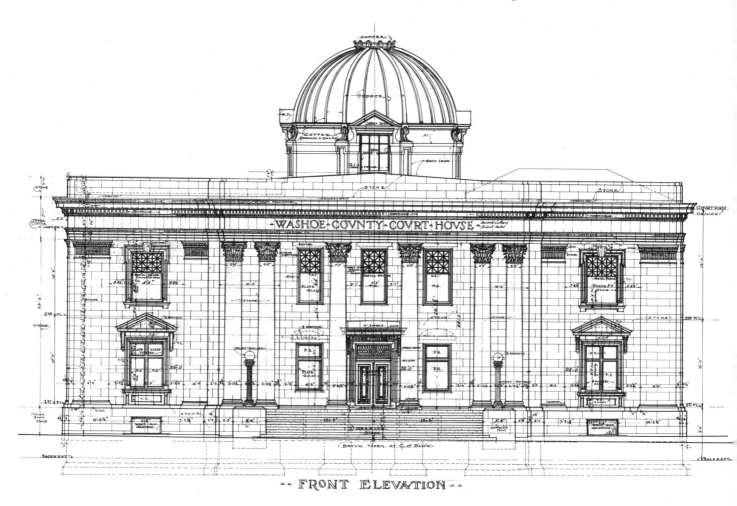

-- FRONT ELEVATION --

The Beaux-Arts façade for DeLongchamps's 1909 Washoe County Courthouse included a raised basement, detailed cornice, heavy columns, clearly articulated parts, and a grand entry. (The DeLongchamps Collection, Getchell Library, University of Nevada, Reno)

what the Washoe County commissioners intended: The structure stepped away from the nineteenth century and was one of the most avant-guard courthouses ever built in Nevada. The county gave the Sellman brothers, who later completed the Elko County Courthouse in 1911, a $250,000 contract for its construction.

Work on the new courthouse, which incorporated parts of the old structure, began in 1909. The building site, on the south side of the Truckee River, was no longer an issue as it had been for the first Reno courthouse; the town had begun extending to the south. Officials laid the cornerstone on June 15, 1910, and dedicated their new facility one year later on June 1, 1911. The two-story stone-clad courthouse continues to serve the county. It has highly ornate features that include a massive copper dome with ribs. Corinthian columns support a two-story portico. Pilasters separate windows that feature terra-cotta surrounds. The first-story windows are pedimented with brackets and projecting sills while those above are capped with a square molding and a central keystone. In the interior there are gray marble wainscotting and pilasters with a black marble base, an elaborate iron balustrade, and multicolor tile floors decorating the halls of both stories. The entrance hall is accented by two flat marble columns. Windows in the copper dome illuminate a spectacular shallow dome of colored, leaded glass that serves as the ceiling for the second-floor hall. This, DeLongchamps's first courthouse, is also his most ornate.[8]

The Washoe County Courthouse soon acquired notoriety as the place where Nevada's liberal divorce law was most frequently implemented. Reno won national fame as a divorce capital after a succession of increasingly lenient, early twentieth-century laws made a Nevada divorce relatively quick and restriction free. Reno, the state's predominant community at the time, with its county courthouse frequently became the center of national attention as the rich and famous made pilgrimages to shed matrimonial bonds.

Shortly after the completion of the courthouse, the Washoe County commission began

DeLongchamps's first courthouse design for Washoe County called for ornate Corinthian columns and iron balustrades. The substantial 1911 Neo-Classical building remains one of Reno's most significant historic structures. (Photo ca. 1911; courtesy of the Nevada Historical Society)

A column from the courtroom of the Washoe County Courthouse dates to the 1911 construction of the building. (Ronald M. James)

considering ways to expand available office space—a search that continues to the present. The additions to the Washoe County Courthouse provide vivid illustrations of the contrast between the modern period of courthouse construction and the previous era. In the 1940s the Washoe County commissioners asked DeLongchamps and his partner, George O'Brien, to design several additions to the 1911 courthouse. Their first two, a north wing (1946) and a south wing (1949), were compatible with the original structure. Although these new wings provided more space for

The cathedral glass ceiling of the Washoe County Courthouse is the most elaborate of its kind in Nevada.
(Ronald M. James)

county use, there soon was a need for still more room. In the 1950s the commissioners once again asked DeLongchamps and O'Brien to design yet another addition. The firm produced several plans, one of which even called for the demolition of the entire complex. Finally, in 1963, the county pursued one of the alternatives and erected a massive annex behind the original courthouse.[9]

The 1963 addition to the Washoe County Courthouse differs dramatically from the original structure. Its green concrete walls rise three stories above the smaller Beaux-Arts building. Not only size distinguishes the two, however. Unlike the original DeLongchamps courthouse,

The 1911 courtroom of the Washoe County Courthouse retains much of its original character.
(Ronald M. James)

which is easily recognizable as a public building, the 1963 annex by his architectural firm is devoid of monumental proportions. Built strictly for practical purposes, it relies on the original 1910 structure to be the ceremonial entrance to the complex.

18 : WHITE PINE COUNTY

White Pine County erected three courthouses. The first, in Hamilton, burned before details of its design could be preserved in the historical record. The second was a temporary structure in Ely, and the third was an expression of monumental architecture that was eclectic in style and reflected the remoteness of mining boomtowns.

Hamilton was a young mining town better known for desperados than for stability. The rush to the silver strikes of the White Pine Mining District, in the late 1860s, contributed to a sudden population explosion that became the basis for the creation of the county on April 1, 1869. Hamilton expanded rapidly, and not surprisingly, its first wooden structure was a saloon.

Eventually, the city fathers perceived the need for additional permanent buildings to improve the image of the town. Russell R. Elliott points out that they

> organized a school district, elected a board of trustees, dedicated a lot for a school house, and fixed the salary of the "school marm" without having so much as a single child in the place. But as one of them remarked when approached with the fact, "Children are a natural thing, they'll come later."[1]

The commissioners were similarly inspired to pursue the construction of a courthouse soon after the organization of their county. They evidently felt that $55,000 was not too high a price to pay for a permanent symbol of law and order. Like the public school system, the new two-story 40 x 60-foot brick courthouse stood ready in 1870 to defy those who would characterize Hamilton as a lawless, uncivilized place.[2]

Hamilton's fortunes declined during the 1870s, while the mining community of Cherry Creek to the northeast was growing, albeit sporadically, and attracted people from Hamilton throughout the decade. In 1880 residents of Cherry Creek began to call for a county-seat shift, and although most of the population of the county came to reside there, the investment of public funds in Hamilton, in the form of the courthouse itself, weakened the clamor for the move. In addition, the people of Ward, a community not large enough to rival Cherry Creek but substantial enough to make its presence known, did not wish to see the seat moved farther away. They called, in one of the rare instances in the state, for a centrally located county seat. Throughout the early 1880s Hamilton diminished in size, and its hold on county government became more difficult to justify. Mail and stage service diminished, and its ability to communicate with the residents of the county grew nearly impossible. Still, White Pine County commissioners resisted attempts to move the seat of government. The disagreement in the county's population, over the selection of a new county seat, encouraged dissension in the legislative delegation and made the state's resolution of the problem impossible to obtain. Hamilton's chess game with the other residents of the county appeared to have reached a stalemate, and in the midst of the maneuvering, the fortunes of Cherry Creek began to decline as did the demand for a county-seat removal.

All this changed on January 6, 1885, when the courthouse in Hamilton burned. The exact cause of the fire remained officially undetermined, even though it appeared to have been arson. The *White Pine News* asserted that the cost of the uninsured building "exceeded that of any like building in Nevada."[3] While standing, it inhibited the shift in government. After the fire, Hamilton was vulnerable to yet another county-seat removal attempt. This time, however, there was no clear inheritor of the prize. Eventually, sufficient support grew for a move to Ely, a young, centrally located mining community, and in 1887 the state legislature authorized the transfer accordingly.[4] As was often the case, county officials rushed into courthouse construction to secure title to the government seat. At the same time, some citizens from Hamilton filed an injunction to prevent the sale of bonds for the Ely courthouse construction and to protest the shift of government. The attempt to block the courthouse failed and construction of the building proceeded.[5]

Unfortunately for the people of White Pine County, the regional economy was depressed in the mid-1880s. County officials could only authorize, therefore, approximately $10,000 for a one-story wooden structure. Morrill John Curtis, Reno architect and builder, submitted his plans for the courthouse to be built on land donated by the Canton Mining Company. Curtis, referred to by Alfred R. Doten as the "university architect," designed Morrill Hall, the first building on the University of Nevada campus in Reno. It was shortly after this project that the architect turned his attention to the White Pine County Courthouse. Curtis was also responsible for designing the Overland Hotel in Reno, the Reno City Hall, the State Insane Asylum, the State

Bank and Trust Company, the Mizpah Hotel in Tonopah, and the Goldfield Hotel and the Nixon Block in Goldfield. A native of Vermont, Curtis came to Nevada at an early age, and died in 1921 at seventy-two.[6]

White Pine County awarded the construction contract for the 34 x 70-foot courthouse to Jacob C. Moon on September 18, 1887, and James Ostergard supervised the work for the county.[7] Although the building was simple in scale, the elegant pedimented gable over the main entrance, the pedimented details over the front door, and the two windows on the front façade bore the mark of Curtis—a professional architect working within the limited means of a meager budget. The structure had a stone foundation, a tin roof, and a fireproof vault in the rear. The *White Pine News* boasted that the courthouse was "a good, substantial structure, sufficient for the wants of this county for many years to come . . . [and] the cheapest building of the kind ever constructed in this State."[8] It was, however, a temporary, modest building intended to house local government officials until the time when the county could erect an impressive courthouse, which would project an image of success and prosperity. Opportunity arrived with the turn-of-the-century copper-mining boom, and the county did not miss the chance to upgrade its image.

Only twenty years after the completion of the previous public facility, White Pine County began work on a new, grander courthouse in Ely. The plan called for a monumental focal point for the community, perched atop a hill overlooking a parklike setting. George T. Beardslee, the architect, supervised the construction of the courthouse, and like many others of the period, the building exhibited an eclectic style of architecture—combining Neo-Classical and Italianate elements. In 1908 the commissioners awarded a contract to R. E. Dodson and G. W. Weller, for $49,699, to build the new courthouse next to the old one.[9]

During construction, county commissioners considered the idea of crowning the building with a copper dome. They regarded the initial bids as too expensive, but after negotiations with the builders the county amended Dodson's and Weller's contract and added $3,384 to include the

White Pine County eventually moved the wooden nineteenth-century courthouse in the background to the east where it became part of a hospital complex. The eclectic-stone structure in the foreground replaced it in 1907. (Photo ca. 1908; Nevada Historical Society)

construction of the dome. The building design was also modified with the substitution of a pressed steel ceiling instead of plaster. The county accepted the building on August 16, 1909.[10] The White Pine County Courthouse is a massive two-story structure of dressed ashlar supported by a raised basement of poured concrete. The symmetrical building rises to a shallow-hipped roof that is banded by a low parapet with a simple, projecting cornice with dentils. A single-story rectangular cupola dominates the structure's roof line. The courthouse includes windows, and the dome and a flagpole, which added to its cost. A pedimented gable and a second-floor balcony over the main entrance highlight the front elevation together with a slightly projecting pedimented gable pavilion. Shallow pilasters grace the corners of the building. The interior of the rectangular plan includes a central hall, a staircase flanked by offices on the first story, and a second-story courtroom. Although the windows and some of the interior have been changed, the courthouse retains its original strength and grandeur. A two-story jail addition, erected in 1925 and located to the rear of the courthouse, is of contemporary design and clearly distinguishable from the original building.

In 1910 the county dug a small lake in front of the courthouse. It became home for several swans and added to the parklike setting. The county moved the older courthouse down the hill, and after significant modifications, the building served as the public hospital. The site for the White Pine County Courthouse is one of the most pastoral in the state. As with the sites selected later for the courthouses in Pershing and Douglas Counties, the White Pine County commissioners worked toward creating as pleasant an environment for the public facility as possible.

19 : PRESERVING AN UNDERSTANDING OF THE PAST

The courthouse is one of the most powerful visual reminders of the presence of law and order in society. These often unequalled examples of monumental architecture symbolize civilization, stability, and justice. Because they are usually well built, they frequently endure for a long time and come to represent a significant part of a people's heritage.

The thirty-four county courthouses built in Nevada since 1863 mirror the pattern of boom and bust that is the hallmark of the state's economic past. Their architecture preserves the diverse and once-popular styles that reflect the cultural and economic climate of the time. Some Nevada county officials have been dedicated to the preservation of their local courthouse, recognizing that it is an important historic resource and an asset to be cherished and passed on.

Nevertheless, of all the courthouses constructed in Nevada, eleven, or approximately one-third, no longer stand. Many were destroyed by individuals who wanted a new image or found their antique building too small. Clearly, the choice to preserve is often as telling as the decision to construct anew. The communities that chose to demolish their buildings convey messages about the local attitude toward public architecture.

Of the destroyed courthouses, three fell victim to fire; eight were purposefully demolished, and of these only two were lost in response to a county-seat move. Table 1 lists the average life span of courthouses for each of the current Nevada county seats—information useful in understanding how communities have dealt with their courthouses. Unfortunately, the table skews the information slightly in a number of ways. It does not take into consideration the county-seat changes that caused several courthouses to be abandoned or demolished. Typically, county-seat transfers reflect economic and demographic conditions, and these have little to do with the conflict between the desire to preserve the old structure or the aspiration to project a certain image with a newer courthouse. Nonetheless, the effect on the data is minimal since most controversies surrounding county-seat moves were settled within the first fifty years of the state's history, thus allowing us to evaluate county actions from that time period to the present. In addition, only one former county seat, Stillwater, built two courthouses and this occurred because of the local government's failure to secure title for the first structure. Given the expense and embarrassment of building on private property and then of needing to replace the courthouse with one on public land, it is reasonable to conclude that the county would have preferred to have built only one. Since all the other former county seats of Nevada had only one courthouse, omitting them from Table 1 does not dramatically affect the impression it provides.

Table 1 does not directly identify the places where people decided to preserve their past nor does it indicate that a feeling of history is stronger in Eureka than in Fallon, for example. There are a number of factors that come into play when a community makes a choice to retain, demolish, or replace a courthouse. The decision underscores a variety of local issues that are tied to the economy and societal and cultural norms. Many of the county seats, which retained their structures for a shorter length of time, have mitigating circumstances that are not clearly portrayed by calculating the average life span of the structures. County officials in Austin (Lander), Pioche (Lincoln), Ely (White Pine), and Fallon (Churchill) all found the need to replace their courthouses, but they reused the existing structure, thus demonstrating either a need for economy or a sense for and a value of history. The 1874 Humboldt County Courthouse in

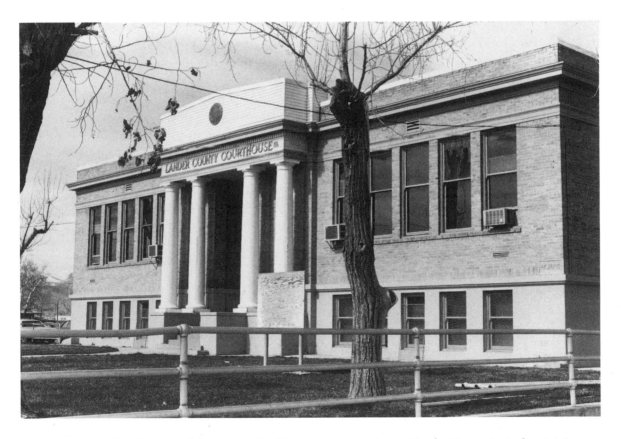

Lander County officials adapted this 1916 school for use as a courthouse. Battle Mountain is the state's most recently designated county seat. (Kathryn M. Kuranda)

TABLE 1

Average Life Span of Courthouses Constructed in Current County Seats as of 1993

Community/County	No. of Courthouses	Average Life Span[1]
Virginia City/Storey	1	117
Eureka/Eureka	1	113
Tonopah/Nye	1	88
Goldfield/Esmeralda	1	85
Yerington/Lyon	1	81
Minden/Douglas	1	77
Lovelock/Pershing	1	72
Carson City/Ormsby	1	71
Elko/Elko	2	62
Reno/Washoe	2	60
Pioche/Lincoln	2	60[2]
Winnemucca/Humboldt	2	60[4]
Austin/Lander	2	59[2]
Hawthorne/Mineral	2	55[3]
Ely/White Pine	2	53[2]
Fallon/Churchill	2	45[2]
Las Vegas/Clark	3	28
State-wide average		67

1. The life span of the courthouses was determined by counting the number of years from the date of the first courthouse construction in each seat and dividing it by the number of courthouses built in each locality. Because the government of Lander County recently moved from Austin to Battle Mountain, it was more appropriate to use the Austin figures, where the government seat resided for over a hundred years, to understand Lander County attitudes.

2. Courthouse replaced, not demolished, and used for other purposes.

3. Original courthouse not demolished, but also not reused.

4. Original courthouse destroyed by fire.

Winnemucca was the victim of fire, but there were attempts to rehabilitate its gutted shell. The well-tended courthouse that replaced it, however, has since acquired historic significance.

The communities that retained their courthouses the longest were mining boomtowns that have not faced subsequent county-seat shift attempts. In addition, lacking a vibrant economy during most of their existence, these counties did not have the financial resources to replace their courthouses. The boom-bust economy of mining necessitated the retention of these buildings, and so it would be inaccurate to suggest that preservation was consistently the result of a concern for maintaining history. It seems more likely that the courthouses continued to exist because of the economic depression that restricted the communities during time periods when officials might have striven to build anew.

Yerington (Lyon), Minden (Douglas), Lovelock (Pershing), and Carson City all have seats of government in communities where the local mentality is distinct from those in mining towns. Yerington, Minden, and Lovelock are agriculturally based and Carson City is the state capital. All have stable populations that in general appear to have developed an appreciation of the past. Although Carson City was late in building a courthouse, like the others it constructed only one and has since been devoted to preserving it.

The remaining county seats have considered different factors in deciding whether to preserve or demolish. The history of Austin is reminiscent of the other four mining boomtowns that have courthouses with long average life spans. The county moved its first courthouse, which was probably never intended to be more than a temporary facility, from Jacobsville to Austin. Upon completion of its replacement in 1872, the community acquired a courthouse that it has used to the present. Although the seat of government recently moved to Battle Mountain, Austin's courthouse continues to provide space for regional county offices. As with Austin, Ely's first courthouse was probably intended to serve temporarily. Upon completion of its monumental successor in 1909, the county decided to move and reused the original modest building.

Churchill County officials made a similar choice after erecting their new facility in 1973. The 1904 courthouse serves as an important ceremonial entry into the county complex. The original 1872 Lincoln County Courthouse in Pioche now serves as a local museum. Although the fate of Mineral County's 1883 courthouse has yet to be determined, it remains standing.

Elko, Reno, and Las Vegas fall into yet another category. Each purposefully demolished a

A glass and steel porch encloses the state's only Romanesque Revival entrance to a county courthouse. The structure is still used by Nye County officials in Tonopah. (Kathryn M. Kuranda)

substantial courthouse to make way for a new structure. These communities apparently felt the need for a program of architectural renewal and had the economic resources to accomplish it. Thus, Elko County demolished its 1869 courthouse after the turn of the century. Shortly after the completion of the 1911 Elko County Courthouse, a local newspaper called for its replacement by an even grander building. Whether because of economics or community choice, this never occurred.

Washoe County incorporated portions of the nineteenth-century courthouse into its 1911 facility. Within forty years, the commissioners considered several plans for its demolition and

DeLongchamps is responsible for this 1963 addition to the Washoe County Courthouse, which he had designed over fifty years before. (Ronald M. James)

replacement. Although they constructed a gargantuan annex, they did retain the core of the original courthouse.

While Clark County is similar to Elko and Washoe Counties in having demolished an earlier facility, this southernmost county has in fact destroyed two, and in its comparatively brief history it is unique because it has accomplished this more quickly than any other county in Nevada. Its courthouses consequently have a brief average life span. Clark County's first build-

Clark County began constructing its third courthouse with the DeLongchamps structure in the background in 1958. The older 1914 structure no longer exists. (Photo dated September 19, 1958; courtesy of Clark County and the Nevada Historical Society)

ing, dating to 1909, was obviously temporary and its replacement predictable. A new courthouse was built five years later, in 1914, with a substantial DeLongchamps design. When the county also replaced this structure, the building had survived only forty-five years, and Las Vegas became the only seat of government in Nevada to have erected three courthouses. All this is made even more striking by the fact that its most recent courthouse underwent major modifications before it was thirty years old. There can be no question that this pattern is partly a response to economic prosperity and mushrooming population growth. It perhaps also points to the distinctive mentality of Las Vegas, grounded as it is in the gaming industry.

Although Nevada in general is famous for its legalized gambling, no other community in the state has been as clearly tied to the industry as Las Vegas. One of the hallmarks of gaming is its need to renovate. Casinos undergo repeated rehabilitations, redecoration programs, and general face-lifts, because new is better, and old is tacky. Las Vegas, more than any other Nevada community, appears to have taken on this point of view. Historic resources are rare in Las Vegas partly because in the past buildings were often seen as good candidates for demolition after only a few decades. This has affected the local architecture, particularly that of public buildings. Consequently, the history of courthouse demolition and construction in Las Vegas is a clear expression of local character.

In at least this one respect, the example of Las Vegas is not unique. Each of Nevada's county courthouses reflects local history. As valuable as documents in an archive, the courthouses speak about a past that created them and in some cases saw their collapse. While not all have fared equally well, most of the survivors remain as symbols of community aspirations and as objects of pride.

In contrast with the endemic wish to build anew, there is a more subtle, insidious threat facing Nevada's county courthouses. This is rooted in the trend to replace the courthouses with sprawling county complexes. These building projects have not, in themselves, jeopardized the future of the courthouse. Such diverse county seats as Reno, Hawthorne, and Virginia City have law enforcement centers separate from their courthouses. In addition, annexes exist in many counties, but the older facilities continue to serve as ceremonial entrances to the county government. Plans to augment existing offices and courtrooms with new buildings in Tonopah and in Reno appear to include the continued use of existing courthouses. There is, however, a danger that county leaders will lose interest in the older building that the community once proudly regarded as its architectural focal point. The agency administrators and elected officials housed in annexes, or in buildings separated from the courthouse, have little interest in seeing the older structure maintained or in having portions of their meager county budgets dedicated to retrofitting the courthouse.

Carson City serves as a dramatic example. Rented space houses most of its offices in the northern part of the community. A law enforcement facility stands in the eastern part of Carson City, with the juvenile courts to the south. The old Ormsby County Courthouse at the center of town remains in use, but the local government will probably pursue plans to sell it to the state. Of course the state will likely maintain the building as an addition to the Capitol Complex, but the community will surrender its only attempt at an architectural centerpiece. The relocation of county offices will continue the century-long tendency for the state government to dominate Carson City. In any other Nevada county seat, where state government would almost certainly not come to the rescue, such a transition would typically result in the abandonment and, eventually, the demolition of the courthouse.

Besides casting a shadow over the future of Nevada's grand historic courthouses, the transition to offices and courts removed from a community's center has an effect on the people's relationship to government. The local government, from its decision-making process to its many offices, is readily accessible, and people frequently interact with their locally elected officials and rely on the services of county government. But for most of us, contact with the judicial process is rare. When the courts were in the center of town, side by side with other government offices and the commission's meeting room, exposure to and familiarity with the courts was commonplace. Today safety issues and the reality of population growth make such proximity less practical, and it is unfortunate to see this important aspect of government and democracy moving further from the people it serves.

In spite of the changes in architectural trends and the nature of government, most of Nevada's county courthouses have nonetheless survived. They are, after all, important expressions of heritage and the most significant symbols of local government and law. In keeping with nationwide practice, Nevadans have generally invested considerable public resources in the construction of these dignified buildings to house their institutions of democracy, justice, and service. It is not surprising, therefore, that Nevadans usually act as responsible custodians as they care for these symbols and pass them on to posterity.

NOTES

INTRODUCTION

1. Angel, *History*, 497.

2. It is increasingly difficult to make a distinction between *new* courthouse projects and new wings or additions to *existing* courthouses. For example, the Humboldt County Courthouse annex in Winnemucca, which does not have a formal, monumental entrance, is not included here as a replacement for the old courthouse because it does not have a ceremonial function for the county complex. On the other hand, the new structure in Fallon does have a monumental entrance, and so it is included as a new courthouse construction even though the original 1904 Churchill County Courthouse remains in use and continues to serve architecturally in a ceremonial capacity. The distinction between "new courthouse" and "county office building" is a subjective call at best, particularly with newer design trends that place less emphasis on monumental architecture.

3. Larson, "Vernacular," 58.

4. Ibid., 57.

5. For one of the best overviews of the region's architectural history, even though by its nature it is necessarily cursory, see Durham, *The Smithsonian Guide*.

6. Stanyer, *County Government in England and Wales*.

7. Snider, *Local Government*, 37.

8. Trillin, "Temples of Democracy."

9. See Wager, *County Government Across the Nation*; Schellenberg, *Conflict*; Duncombe, *County Government in America*; and Snider, *Local Government*.

1 : JUSTICE IN BALANCE: DESIGN, SYMBOL & HISTORY

1. See Thomas Carter and Peter Goss, *Utah's Historic Architecture, 1847–1940: A Guide* (Salt Lake City: University of Utah Press, 1988); and Jennifer Eastman Attebery, *Building Idaho: An Architectural History* (Moscow: University of Idaho Press, 1991).

2. Hitchcock and Seale, *Temples of Democracy*.

3. National Trust, *Courthouse*, 9.

4. Lounsbury, "The Structure of Justice," 219, 226. For a related discussion, see also Girouard, *Cities and People*.

5. Pomeroy, *The Pacific Slope*.

6. Bowen, "Registration Problems," 744–745. For a history of the architectural profession, see Briggs, *The Architect in History*.

7. "The DeLongchamps Collection," Special Collections, Getchell Library, University of Nevada, Reno; Geier, "Frederick J. DeLongchamps, Reno's Architect"; Datin, "The Man Who Built Reno"; Nylen, "Reno's Premier Architect"; *Reno Nevada State Journal* 12 February 1969; *Artemisia, University of Nevada Yearbook*; Boyd Moore, *Persons in the Foreground: Nevada*.

8. Adkins, "Coming into its Own."

9. National Trust, *Courthouse,* 9.

10. Robinson, *The People's Architecture,* x. Besides this text, other examples of statewide courthouse surveys include: Dreyfuss, *A History of Arizona's Counties and Courthouses;* Rayfield, Welch, and Nance, *The Texas Courthouse;* Brady, *County Courthouses of Oklahoma;* Hollander, "County Courthouses of New Mexico"; Gurney, *Mississippi Courthouses;* Trillin, "Temples"; Kelly, "America's Historic Courthouses"; and Hall, "The Kansas Courthouses of George P. Washburn, Architect."

11. The state has had only sixteen counties since Ormsby County and Carson City were consolidated into a single municipal government by a constitutional amendment election in 1968. Carson City-Ormsby County is, nevertheless, treated fully here. Bullfrog County, created in 1987 and abolished in 1989, was never intended to function as a normal county and is not presented in this discussion.

12. Larson, "Vernacular," 57.

13. Larson points out that "one can identify diffusion ripples spreading westward. Thus, as late as 1871, a modest Greek Revival courthouse was built in [Lander County] Nevada." Ibid.

14. For an excellent overview of styles, see Whiffen, *American Architecture.*

15. Ibid., 38–47. For examples of Greek Revival houses, see also "Historic Property Survey Report and Multiple Resource Area Nomination to the National Register of Historic Places for Carson City, Nevada" (report on file at the Nevada State Historic Preservation Office, Carson City, Nevada, 1980).

16. *Eureka Sentinel,* 13 September 1871, quoted from the *Reese River Reveille,* 8 September 1871.

17. Greeley, *An Overland Journey,* 230–231.

18. Whiffen, *American Architecture,* 97–102.

19. Schellenberg, *Conflict;* see also Paher, *Significant.*

20. Larson, "Vernacular," 58.

21. Whiffen, *American Architecture,* 213–216.

22. Ibid., 167–172.

23. Ibid., 225–228.

24. National Trust, *Courthouse,* 10.

25. Larson, "Vernacular," 59.

26. For a discussion of pragmatism and the cult of thrift and its influence on public architecture, see Hitchcock and Seale, *Temples of Democracy.*

2 : CARSON CITY & ORMSBY COUNTY

1. The use of this name in the area predates Curry's plat. Carson County was a Utah Territorial designation for much of the western Great Basin in the early 1850s.

2. Del Papa, *Political History of Nevada,* 69ff; Angel, *History,* 550ff; *Carson City Nevada Tribune,* 22 July 1876.

3. Minutes of the board of the Ormsby County Commission, vol. 1, 13, and 14, October 13, 1862.

4. Angel, *History,* 543.

5. *Carson City Daily Appeal,* 28 March 1878.

6. "DeLongchamps Collection," Special Collections, Getchell Library, University of Nevada, Reno.

7. *Carson City Daily Appeal,* 25 February 1921.

8. Ibid., 1 March 1920.

9. Ibid., 16 March 1920. In 1993 the Nevada State Historic Preservation Office conducted a preliminary review of what appears to be the remains of the demolition. Burnt timbers and construction

rubble confirm the drastic measures described in the primary documents.

10. Ibid., 21 August 1920.

11. Ibid., 15 March 1922.

12. A new supreme court building opened in the Capitol Complex in 1992. The former facility provides room for an expansion of the attorney general's offices.

3 : CHURCHILL COUNTY

1. H. R. Whitchall, *Biennial Report of the State Mineralogist of the State of Nevada* (Carson City: State Printer, 1871, 1872), 14. See also *Virginia City Territorial Enterprise*, 8 November 1867, 16 January 1872.

2. Marcia de Braga, *Graves*, 26. See also, Angel, *History*, 364 ff.

3. Townley, *Turn this Water into Gold*, 8, 13, 14; and de Braga, *Graves*, 26.

4. See minutes of the board of the Churchill County Commission; *Fallon Standard*, 13 August 1941; Edaburn, "County Seats on the Move"; and *Las Vegas Review-Journal*, 14 August 1966.

5. Churchill County Courthouse proposal; "The DeLongchamps Collection" Special Collections, Getchell Library, University of Nevada, Reno.

4 : CLARK COUNTY

1. Hulse, *Lincoln County*, 78–80.

2. Paher, *Las Vegas*, 105–111; Jones and Cahlan, *Water*, 38–39, 50–51, 88, 92. See also, the *Las Vegas Age*, 17 April 1909.

3. *Las Vegas Age*, 9 August 1913.

4. Ibid., 9 August, 1 November, 6 and 13 December 1913; "The DeLongchamps Collection," Special Collections, Getchell Library, University of Nevada, Reno; minutes of the board of the Clark County Commission.

5. *Las Vegas Age*, 9 August 1913.

6. Ibid., 24 January 1914.

7. Ibid., 21 November 1914.

8. Ibid., 12 December 1914.

9. Ibid.

10. Ibid.

11. For a discussion on how growth has affected public architecture, see Hitchcock and Seale, *Temples of Democracy*, 265–302.

12. For a discussion of the history of gambling and its effects on the image, growth, and mentality of Las Vegas, see Findlay, *People of Chance*.

13. See bid documents, plans, and specifications at the Clark County Courthouse; and also Hughes, *The Shock of the New*, 164–211.

14. Venturi, Scott Brown, and Izenour, *Learning*, 107.

15. Wolfe, *The Kandy-Kolored Tangerine-Flake Streamline Baby*, 8; quoted by Venturi, Scott Brown, and Izenour, *Learning*, 53.

16. Hine, *Populuxe*.

17. Whiffen, *American Architecture*, 275–279.

18. For an overview of the character and history of Las Vegas, see Moehring, *Resort City*; and Shepperson, *Mirage-Land*.

5 : DOUGLAS COUNTY

1. Angel, *History*, 74; *Virginia City Territorial Enterprise*, 13 June 1872.

2. Ibid.; see also Lord, *Comstock Mining*, 101.

3. Angel, *History*, 375.

4. Chapter XLVII of the Third Session, *Laws of Nevada*, approved February 9, 1864.

5. Douglas County Courthouse specifications on file at the Nevada State Historic Preservation Office, Carson City, Nevada.

6. *Douglas County Banner*, 7 October 1865.

7. Douglas County Courthouse specifications on file at the Nevada State Historic Preservation Office, Carson City, Nevada.

8. Angel, *History*.

9. *Douglas County Banner*, 7 October 1865.

10. *Gardnerville Record-Courier*, 14 May, 4 June, 9 July, 15 October, 31 December 1915.

11. Krick, "History of the Douglas County Courthouse," 227ff; *Gardnerville Record-Courier*, 26 March, 14 May, 4 June, 2 July, 9 July, 15 October, 31 December 1915, 24 March 1916.

12. *Gardnerville Record-Courier*, 24 March 1916.

13. Ibid.

6 : ELKO COUNTY

1. He later resigned, perhaps because the quality of the work was found wanting. See Aldrich, "Elko."

2. Ibid.

3. Ninth U.S. Manuscript Census (1870).

4. *Elko Independent*, 17 July 1869.

5. Ibid., 16 and 30 October 1869.

6. Patterson, Ulph, and Goodwin, *Nevada's*, 542–543; *Elko Independent*, 1 and 11 September, 16 and 30 October, 22 and 25 December 1869; and Aldrich, "Elko."

7. See Lewis, *W. H. Weeks, Architect*, 215.

8. *Elko Free Press*, 3 August 1910.

9. "Industrial Issue," *Elko Independent*, August 1916. Other sources include Aldrich, "Elko"; Patterson, *Nevada's*, 542–543; *Elko Free Press*, 3 August 1910.

7 : ESMERALDA COUNTY

1. Angel, *History*, 402ff.

2. This discussion appears in length in Paher, *Significant*, 70–90. See also the *Goldfield Daily Tribune*, 25 January, 2 May 1907; *Goldfield News*, 1 September 1905; and Elliott, *Nevada's Twentieth-Century*, 1–153.

3. See Elliott, *Nevada's Twentieth-Century*, 103ff; and Zanjani and Rocha, *Ignoble Conspiracy*.

4. Shamberger, *Story*; *Goldfield News*, 13 July 1907; *Goldfield Review*, 19 September 1908; *Goldfield Daily Tribune*, 25 January 1905, 19 April 1907.

5. See the Esmeralda County WPA files, MS/NC 278, box 16, folder 8, Nevada Historical Society, Reno, Nevada.

8 : EUREKA COUNTY

1. *Eureka Sentinel*, 25 March 1873.

2. Ibid.

3. Minutes of the board of the Eureka County Commission.

4. *Virginia City Territorial Enterprise*, 29 June 1873.

5. "Jail Plan," Eureka County Courthouse. Photo reproductions of the plans are available at the Nevada Historical Society, Reno, Nevada, and at the

Nevada State Historic Preservation Office, Carson City, Nevada.

6. *Virginia City Territorial Enterprise*, 29 June 1873, taken from the *Eureka Sentinel*, 26 June 1873.

7. *Eureka Sentinel*, 22 April 1879.

8. "Courthouse Plans," Eureka County Courthouse. Photo reproductions of the plans are available at the Nevada Historical Society, Reno, Nevada, and at the Nevada State Historic Preservation Office, Carson City, Nevada.

9. Adkins, "Nevada Architects." Bennett may have been one of the supervising architects for the California State Capitol as identified on a plaque on that building.

10. See Guinn, *Historical*; and Adkins, "Nevada Architects."

11. See *Eureka Daily Leader*, 31 December 1880.

12. See Angel, *History*, 440.

13. *Eureka Sentinel*, 29 May 1880.

14. Ibid.

15. Molinelli, *Eureka*, 14; additional sources include *Eureka Sentinel*, 22 April, 19 May 1879, 2 January 1880; *Virginia City Territorial Enterprise*, 29 June 1873; see also James, "Eureka."

9 : HUMBOLDT COUNTY

1. *Humboldt Register*, 28 July, 1 August, 7 November 1863.

2. Ibid., 1 August 1863.

3. *Unionville Silver State*, 23 March 1872.

4. Ibid., 28 August 1872.

5. Angel, *History*, 458–459.

6. See McDonald, "Early Courthouse"; *Unionville Silver State*, 23 March, 28 and 31 August, 7

September 1872; *Reno Nevada State Journal*, 11 March 1874.

7. Nevertheless, the fire ultimately led to the formation of Pershing County (see chapter 15).

8. *Humboldt Star*, 23 February 1920, 3 January 1921; *Winnemucca Silver State*, 5 April 1919, 19 October 1920, 4 January 1921. See also the *Lovelock Review-Miner*, 26 July 1918.

9. "The DeLongchamps Collection," Special Collections, Getchell Library, University of Nevada, Reno.

10. The National Register nomination for the Humboldt County Courthouse provides an overview of the structure's details and history. See the files of the Nevada State Historic Preservation Office, Carson City, Nevada.

10 : LANDER COUNTY

1. The published bid request in the *Virginia City Territorial Enterprise* (3 April 1863) provides the best extant description of the building. There is, however, the possibility that the structure took a different form in the course of construction. See also the *Eureka Sentinel*, 13 September 1871; Hall, "Austin, Nevada"; and Angel, *History*, 462.

2. *Eureka Sentinel*, 13 September 1871, quoted from the *Reese River Reveille*, 8 September 1871.

3. *Reese River Reveille*, 11 September 1871.

4. *Eureka Sentinel*, 13 September 1871, quoted from the *Reese River Reveille*, 8 September 1871.

5. *Reese River Reveille*, 13 January 1872.

6. *Virginia City Territorial Enterprise*, 31 July 1877.

7. *Reese River Reveille*, 17 November 1871, 17 January 1872.

8. See Paher, "Courthouse on Wheels."

9. *Elko Free Press*, 2 October 1980; *Reno Nevada State Journal*, 22 October 1980, 30 May 1982.

10. Larson, "Vernacular," 57.

11 : LINCOLN COUNTY

1. Hulse, *Lincoln*, 68; minutes of the board of the Lincoln County Commission, vol. 1, 18, and 27; *Pioche Record*, 24 January 1873, 11 February 1874.

2. Angel, *History*, 479–480; *Pioche Record*, 26 October 1872.

3. *Ely Record* (*Lincoln County Record*), 4 September 1872. See also *Pioche Daily Record*, 13 September 1872. Steel was an Odd Fellow, and one of his first projects in Pioche was to erect a stone building for his partner who was a merchant.

4. Hulse, *Lincoln*, 70ff; Angel, *History*, 479–480.

5. *Pioche Record*, 9 January 1873.

6. Ibid., 1 March 1876.

7. Ibid., 3 May 1876.

8. See, for example, Ibid., 16 August 1879, 5 November 1881, 1 June 1889, 2 August 1890.

9. Minutes of the board of the Lincoln County Commission, 1937–1938, research by Sandra Dulgar; Hulse, *Lincoln*, 77–78.

10. Wright, "Las Vegas Hospital."

12 : LYON COUNTY

1. *Gold Hill Daily News*, 17 August 1864.

2. Angel, *History*, 497.

3. *Como Sentinel*, 4 April 1864.

4. *Yerington Times*, 6 May, 23 December 1911, 27 April, 12 October 1912; *Mason Valley News*, 4 February, 15 April, 23 December 1911; "The De-Longchamps Collection," Special Collections, Getchell Library, University of Nevada, Reno.

5. *Yerington Times*, 27 April 1912.

6. The federal government assisted in paying for the addition. See document in the files of the Lyon County Recorder's Office, Yerington, Nevada, dated April 6, 1936. A copy is available in the files of the Nevada State Historic Preservation Office, Carson City, Nevada.

13 : MINERAL COUNTY

1. *Reno Nevada State Journal*, 11 April 1883.

2. Ibid., 15 March 1883. See also 13 July 1883, 11 December 1883.

3. Ibid., 22 January 1884.

4. The evidence for the existence of the cupola comes from a photograph in the files of the Nevada Historical Society in Reno. Because the photograph may be a composite, to see what the cupola looked like, there is some question whether the architectural element ever existed beyond the preliminary plans. County and newspaper records are vague on this point, with the exception of the *Goldfield Tribune*, 2 May 1907.

5. See McInnis, "Courthouse."

6. *Mineral County Independent and Hawthorne News*, 2 October 1968.

7. Ibid., 2 and 30 October 1968, 6 and 20 August 1969, 9 September 1970. See also minutes of the board of the Mineral County Commission, vol. 36–38.

8. See the plans for the Mineral County Court-

house in the files of the Nevada State Historic Preservation Office, Carson City, Nevada.

14 : NYE COUNTY

1. *Gold Hill Daily News*, 6 April 1864.
2. Angel, *History*, 515.
3. *Virginia City Territorial Enterprise*, 21 May 1867; Theron Fox, "Belmont's Other Courthouse," in Paher, *Nevada Official Bicentennial Book*, 303–304. Phillip I. Earl's assertion, as reported in the *Reno Gazette-Journal*, 9 July 1989, that Belmont constructed a simple wooden courthouse before the mid-1870s remains unverified and in question.
4. *Virginia City Territorial Enterprise*, 24 August 1875.
5. Ibid., 20 May, 24 November 1875. See also *Carson City Daily Appeal*, 21 March 1875.
6. Ibid., 24 August 1875.
7. Ibid., 21 May 1867, 13 July 1875.
8. Elliott, *Nevada's Twentieth-Century Mining Boom*, 60–61.
9. *Tonopah Sun*, 14 April 1905.
10. *Tonopah Bonanza*, 15 April 1905.
11. Ibid., 1 April 1905, 10 June 1905; *Tonopah Sun*, 19 and 21 March 1905.
12. For the Nye County Courthouse plans, see WPA files box 16, folder 30, Nevada Historical Society, Reno, Nevada.

15 : PERSHING COUNTY

1. *Lovelock Review-Miner*, 14 September 1923.
2. McDonald, "Development"; see also minutes of the board of the Pershing County Commission, vol. 1; and Nevada Revised Statutes 243,330, chap. 62 of the Statutes of Nevada, 1919, 75–82.
3. Minutes of the board of the Pershing County Commission, vol. 1. The Pershing Hotel was not even one year old at the time. See the *Lovelock Review-Miner*, 1 April 1919.
4. *Lovelock Review-Miner*, 17 October 1919.
5. *Winnemucca Silver State*, 5 April 1919, 19 October 1920, 4 January 1921; *Humboldt Star*, 9 August 1918, 23 February 1920, 3 January 1921.
6. *Lovelock Review-Miner*, 12 December 1919, 14 September 1923.
7. Ibid., 17 October 1919.
8. This was the consensus of meetings with Pershing County residents in Lovelock on October 27, 1985, and January 21, 1986; see minutes of the board of the Pershing County Commission, vol. 1, December 5, 1919.
9. *Lovelock Review-Miner*, 12 December 1919.
10. Ibid., 7 May 1920, 14 September 1923.
11. Ibid., 26 March 1920.
12. The Nevada State Historic Preservation Office contacted its counterparts in other states during 1985 and 1986 to determine whether there were other round courthouses in the nation. Texas has four nearly round courthouses built on a cruciform design.
13. *Lovelock Review-Miner*, 26 March 1920, 10 and 21 June 1921; see also minutes of the board of the Pershing County Commission; and "The DeLongchamps Collection," Special Collections, Getchell Library, University of Nevada, Reno.

16 : STOREY COUNTY

1. *Virginia City Territorial Enterprise*, 3 July 1873.

2. See Kirker, *California's Architectural,* 209; and Adkins, "Nevada Architects," 44.

3. *Virginia City Territorial Enterprise,* 25 June 1876. Alternative plans for the courthouse are on display at the Storey County recorder's office.

4. *Virginia City Territorial Enterprise,* 5 December 1875.

5. For records concerning the statue of Justice, see the files related to the construction of the building in the clerk's office of the Storey County Courthouse. Duplicates of the plans for the building are available in the Nevada State Historic Preservation Office, Carson City, Nevada.

6. *Gold Hill Daily News,* 12 June 1876. See also McDonald, "House," 343–344.

7. Simmonds, "Blindfold," 1164; Pome, *Pantheon,* 232–234; and Tooke, *Pantheon,* 388.

8. Correspondence with state historic preservation officers and additional sources identified two statues of Justice without a blindfold in California, two in Colorado, one in Iowa, five in Kansas, one in Louisiana, four in Michigan, two in Oregon (one surviving), one in North Carolina, two in North Dakota, three in Pennsylvania (two surviving), and three in Texas; see also "The New Sessions House," *The Building News and Engineering Journal,* 91, 2700 (October 6, 1906), 459.

9. The receipt is part of the collection of documents related to the courthouse construction on file in the Storey County Courthouse, Virginia City, Nevada.

10. *Virginia City Territorial Enterprise,* 18 February 1877.

11. Drury, *Editor,* 161–162; *Virginia City Territorial Enterprise,* 1 July 1897.

17 : WASHOE COUNTY

1. Angel, *History,* 625ff; *Reno Nevada State Journal,* 16 April 1873.

2. See John M. Townley, *Tough Little Town on the Truckee,* History of Reno Series, vol. 1 (Reno: Great Basin Studies Center, 1983); and Rowley, *Reno.*

3. Paher, *Significant,* 39. See also Angel, *History,* 626–627.

4. For an excellent overview of the Washoe County seat shift and the controversy associated with the location of the courthouse in Reno, see Paher, *Significant,* 8–40. See also the *Reno Nevada State Journal,* 15 July 1871.

5. Angel, *History,* 627. See also *Reno Nevada State Journal,* 22 June 1872.

6. *Reno Nevada State Journal,* 16 April 1873.

7. Ibid., 12 March 1873.

8. *Reno Evening Gazette,* 28 August 1909, 1 and 2 June 1911; *Reno Nevada State Journal,* 20 December 1909, 1 and 14 June, 21 and 23 November 1910, 29 January, 1 and 23 May, 1 and 7 June 1911; "The DeLongchamps Collection," Getchell Library, University of Nevada, Reno; Davidson, "Washoe," 139–144; Lawrence-Dietz, "Washoe," 1–2.

9. "The DeLongchamps Collection," Special Collections, Getchell Library, University of Nevada, Reno.

18 : WHITE PINE COUNTY

1. Elliott, *Early History,* 23.

2. Angel, *History,* 650. See also "White Pine

County Courthouse," *Nevada Magazine* 4, 5 (January 1949).

3. *White Pine News*, 20 January 1885.

4. Paher, *Significant*, 99–125. See also *White Pine News*, 10 and 17 January 1885.

5. Ibid., 7 January 1888.

6. *Reno Evening Gazette*, 6 October 1887. Although occasionally appearing as John Morrill Curtis, this is almost certainly the same person. *Reno Nevada State Journal*, 25 and 26 January 1921. See also Doten, *Journals*; and Koval, "Goldfield Hotel."

7. *White Pine News*, 16 April 1887, 16 July 1887, 7 January 1888. See also Read, *White Pine Lang Syne*, 271. The specifications called for redwood shingles, but this was apparently changed.

8. *White Pine News*, 7 January 1888.

9. Transcription of minutes of the board of the White Pine County Commission by Susan Reck are available in the Nevada State Historic Preservation Office, Carson City, Nevada.

10. Ibid. See also *White Pine News*, 12 February, 7, 8, and 15 April, 6 and 20 May, 20 and 30 June, 1 July 1908.

GLOSSARY

1. See *The American Heritage Dictionary of the English Language*. 3rd ed. (Boston: Houghton Mifflin Co., 1992).

GLOSSARY[1]

arch. A structural device, especially of masonry, forming the curved, pointed, or flat upper edge of an open space and supporting the weight above it, as in a bridge or doorway.

architrave. The lowermost part of an entablature that rests directly on top a column.

base. The lowest or bottom part of a structure, as a wall, considered as a separate architectural unit.

capital. The top part, or head, of a pillar or column.

cartouche. A scroll-like tablet used either to provide space for an inscription or for ornamental purposes.

column. A supporting pillar consisting of a base, a cylindrical shaft, and a capital.

corbel. A bracket of stone, wood, brick, or other building material, projecting from the face of a wall and generally used to support a cornice or an arch.

Corinthian. The most ornate of the classical orders of architecture, characterized by a slender fluted column having an ornate bell-shaped capital decorated with acanthus leaves.

cornice. A horizontal molded projection that crowns or completes a building or wall. The uppermost part of an entablature.

dentils. One of a series of small rectangular blocks forming a molding or projecting beneath a cornice.

Doric order. The oldest and simplest Greek architectural order.

entablature. The upper section of a classical building, resting on the capital and including the architrave.

finial. An ornament fixed to the peak of an arch or arched structure.

fluting. A decorative motif consisting of a series of long, rounded, parallel grooves, such as those incised in the surface of a column.

frieze. A plain or decorated horizontal part of an entablature between the architrave.

Ionic order. An order of classical Greek architecture characterized by two opposed volutes (spiral, scroll-like ornaments) in the capital.

parapet. A low, protective wall or railing along the edge of a roof, balcony, or similar structure.

pilaster. A pillar or column with a capital and base, set into a wall as an ornamental motif.

Tuscan order. A classical order similar to Doric, but having an unfluted shaft with a simplified base, capital, and entablature.

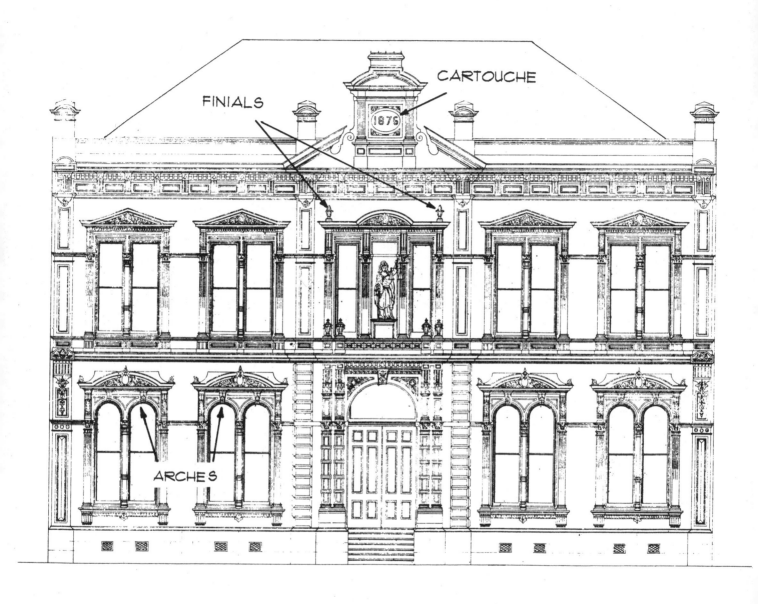

FINIALS

CARTOUCHE

1875

ARCHES

FRONT ELEVATION.

The Kenitzer and Raun plans for the 1875 Storey County Courthouse feature one of the most elaborate Italianate façades completed in Nevada. (Photo by Scott Klette; additions by John Copoulos, architect)

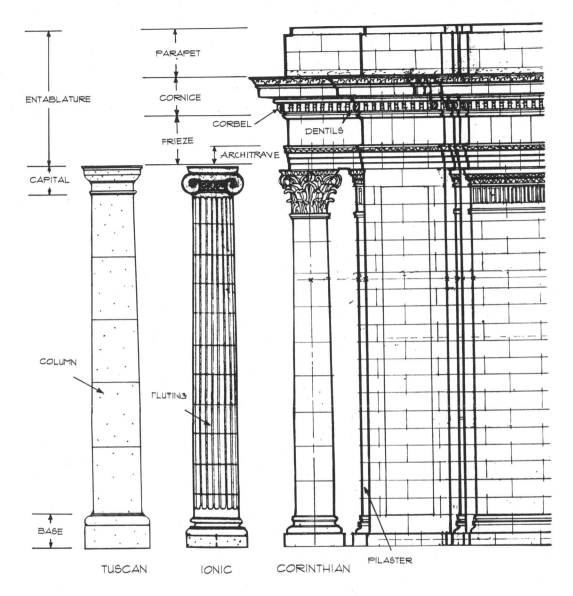

ENTABLATURE

PARAPET

CORNICE

CORBEL

DENTILS

FRIEZE

ARCHITRAVE

CAPITAL

COLUMN

FLUTING

BASE

TUSCAN   IONIC   CORINTHIAN   PILASTER

DeLongchamps's 1909 Washoe County Courthouse features Corinthian columns and the massing of a Neo-Classical structure, which was influenced by the Beaux-Arts movement. (Adapted from the DeLongchamps Collection, Getchell Library, University of Nevada, Reno; with additions by John Copoulos, architect.) Tuscan and Ionic columns from DeLongchamps's plans for the Ormsby and Pershing County Courthouses, respectively. If the Tuscan column from Ormsby County had no base and were fluted (like the Ionic column), it would be called Doric.

BIBLIOGRAPHY

PRIMARY SOURCES AND DOCUMENTS

Angel, Myron F. *History of Nevada with Illustrations and Biographical Sketches of its Prominent Men and Pioneers*. Oakland: Thompson and West, 1881. Reprint, Berkeley: Howell-North, 1958.

Artemisia, University of Nevada Yearbook. Reno: University of Nevada, 1904.

"The DeLongchamps Collection." Special Collections, Getchell Library, University of Nevada, Reno.

Doten, Alfred. *The Journals of Alfred Doten: 1849–1903*. Edited by Walter Van Tilburg Clark. Reno: University of Nevada Press, 1973.

Drury, Wells. *An Editor on the Comstock Lode*. Palo Alto: Pacific Books, 1948.

Greeley, Horace. *An Overland Journey from New York to San Francisco in the Summer of 1859*. New York: C. M. Saxton, Barker Co., 1860. Reprint, New York: Alfred A. Knopf, 1963.

Lord, Eliot. *Comstock Mining and Miners*. Washington, D.C.: U.S. Government Printing Office, 1883. Reprint, Berkeley: Howell-North, 1959.

Molinelli, Lambert, and Company. *Eureka and its Resources*. San Francisco: H. Keller and Company, 1879. Reprint, Reno: University of Nevada Press, 1982.

Moore, Boyd. *Persons in the Foreground: Nevada*. N.p., 1915.

Pome, François Antoine. *The Pantheon: London 1694*. New York: Garland Publishing, Inc., 1976. Reprint, B. Motte, R. Clavel, and C. Harper: 1694; translated by J. A. B.

Tooke, Andrew. *The Pantheon: London 1713*. New York: Garland Publishing, Inc., 1976. Reprint of Tooke's translated adaptation of F. A. Pome's work in 1713 printed by C. Harper.

Wolfe, Tom. *The Kandy-Kolored Tangerine-Flake Streamline Baby*. New York: Farrar, Straus and Giroux, 1965.

ADDITIONAL PRIMARY SOURCES

Minutes of county commission meetings are stored in the courthouses of the respective counties.

Statutes of the State of Nevada provide information on county organization and the funding of courthouse construction.

Plans and specifications for county courthouses are on file at the county courthouses; the Nevada State Historic Preservation Office, Carson City, Nevada; or at the Nevada Historical Society, Reno, Nevada (particularly in the Works Progress Administration [WPA] collection). In addition, "The DeLongchamps Collection" cited includes numerous plans for courthouse construction and alteration.

SECONDARY SOURCES

Adkins, Richard D. "Coming into its Own: Nevada and the Emergence of its Architectural

Profession." Unpublished manuscript on file at the Nevada State Historic Preservation Office, Carson City, Nevada (July 23, 1992).

Adkins, Richard D., Ronald M. James, and Richard A. Bernstein. "Nevada Architects and Builders." In *Nevada Comprehensive Preservation Plan*, edited by William G. White and Ronald M. James. 2nd ed. Carson City: Nevada State Historic Preservation Office, 1991.

Aldrich, Ethel. "Elko County's First Courthouse." *Northeastern Nevada Society Quarterly* 7, no. 3 (Winter 1977).

Bowen, Ian. "Registration Problems." *Architect's Journal* (London) 118 (December 17, 1953).

Brady, Charles. *County Courthouses of Oklahoma.* Edited by Tim Zwink and Gordon Moore. Oklahoma City: Oklahoma Historical Society, 1985.

Briggs, Martin S. *The Architect in History.* Oxford: Clarendon Press, 1927.

Datin, Richard C. "The Man Who Built Reno—and a Lot Else." *Carson City Nevada Appeal,* 17 June 1970.

Davidson, John. "Washoe County Courthouse." *Nevada State Bar Journal* 3, no. 3 (July 1938).

de Braga, Marcia. *Dig No Graves: A History of Churchill County.* Sparks: Western Printing and Publishing, 1964.

Del Papa, Frankie Sue. *Political History of Nevada.* 9th ed. Carson City: Nevada State Printing Office, 1990.

Dreyfuss, John J., ed. *A History of Arizona's Counties and Courthouses.* Tucson: Arizona Historical Society, 1972.

Duncombe, Herbert Sydney. *County Government in America.* Washington, D. C.: National Association of Counties Research Foundation, 1966.

Durham, Michael S. *The Smithsonian Guide to Historic America: The Desert States.* New York: Stewart, Tabori and Chang, 1990.

Edaburn, Sharon L. "County Seats on the Move." Unpublished manuscript on file at the Churchill County Museum, Fallon, Nevada.

Elliott, Russell R. *The Early History of White Pine County, Nevada: 1865–1887.* M.A. thesis, University of Washington, 1938.

——. *Nevada's Twentieth-Century Mining Boom: Tonopah, Goldfield, Ely.* Reno: University of Nevada Press, 1966.

Findlay, John M. *People of Chance: Gambling in American Society from Jamestown to Las Vegas.* New York: Oxford University Press, 1986.

Geier, Corry L. A. "Frederick J. DeLongchamps, Reno's Architect." Unpublished manuscript on file at the Nevada State Historic Preservation Office, Carson City, Nevada (1981).

Girouard, Mark. *Cities and People: A Social and Architectural History.* New Haven: Yale University Press, 1985.

Guinn, J. M. *Historical and Biographical Record of Los Angeles and Vicinity.* Chicago: Chapman Publishing, 1901.

Gurney, Bill. *Mississippi Courthouses.* Ripley: Old Timer Press, 1987.

Hall, Charles L. "The Kansas Courthouses of George P. Washburn, Architect." *Journal of the West* 17, no. 1 (January 1978).

Hall, Shawn R. "Austin, Nevada." *Northeastern Nevada Historical Society Quarterly* no. 4 (1992).

Hine, Thomas. *Populuxe: The Look and Life of*

America in the '50s and '60s, from the Tailfins and TV Dinners to Barbie Dolls and Fallout Shelters. New York: Alfred A. Knopf, 1987.

Hitchcock, Henry-Russell, and William Seale. *Temples of Democracy: The State Capitols of the U.S.A.* New York: Harcourt Brace Jovanovich, 1976.

Hollander, Kate. "County Courthouses of New Mexico." *Preservation New Mexico* 3, no. 3 (Fall 1986).

Hughes, Robert. *The Shock of the New.* New York: Alfred A. Knopf, 1982.

Hulse, James W. *Lincoln County, Nevada: 1864–1909.* Reno: University of Nevada Press, 1971.

James, Steve. "Eureka Historical Buildings and Archeological Project." Report, Nevada Historical Society, Reno, Nevada, and the Nevada State Historic Preservation Office, Carson City, Nevada, 1985.

Jones, Florence Lee, and John F. Cahlan. *Water: A History of Las Vegas.* Vol. 1. Las Vegas: Las Vegas Valley Water District, 1975.

Kelly, Leslie A. "America's Historic Courthouses." *Nissan Discovery* 10, no. 3 (May–June 1986).

Kirker, Harold. *California's Architectural Frontier: Style and Tradition in the Nineteenth Century.* 3rd ed. Layton: Gibbs M. Smith, 1986.

Kostof, Spiro, ed. *The Architect: Chapters in the History of the Profession.* New York: Oxford University Press, 1977.

Koval, Ana B., and Charles D. Zeier. "Goldfield Hotel." National Register of Historic Places nomination, Nevada State Historic Preservation Office, Carson City, Nevada, 1980.

Krick, Grover L. "History of the Douglas County Courthouse." *The Nevada State Bar Journal* 4, no. 3 (July 1939).

Larson, Albert J. "From Vernacular through High-Style: The Ubiquitous American County Courthouse." In *Purposes in Built Form and Culture Research*, edited by J. William Carswell and David G. Saile. Lawrence: University of Kansas Press, 1986.

Lawrence-Dietz, Patricia. "Washoe County Courthouse." *Heritage Herald* 3, no. 5 (May–June 1983).

Lewis, Betty. *W. H. Weeks, Architect.* Fresno: Panorama West Books, 1985.

Lounsbury, Carl. "The Structure of Justice: The Courthouses of Colonial Virginia." In *Perspectives in Vernacular Architecture, III,* edited by Thomas Carter and Bernard L. Herman. Columbia: University of Missouri, 1989.

Lowry, Bates. *Building a National Image: Architectural Drawings for the American Democracy, 1789–1912.* Washington, D.C.: National Building Museum, 1985.

McDonald, Russell W. "The House of Unblindfolded Justice." *American Bar Association Journal* 57 (April 1971).

——. "The Development of Lovelock." *Nevada Historical Society Quarterly* 19, no. 4 (Winter 1976).

——. "Early Courthouse and Lawyers of Humboldt County." *Humboldt Historian* 1, no. 1 (Summer 1978).

McInnis, Helen. "Courthouse served Two Counties." *Nevada State Museum Newsletter* (Fall 1983).

Moehring, Eugene P. *Resort City in the Sunbelt:*

Las Vegas, 1930–1970. Reno: University of Nevada Press, 1989.

Mumford, Lewis. *The Brown Decades: A Study of the Arts in America: 1865–1895*. New York: Dover Publications, 1971.

National Trust for Historic Preservation, *A Courthouse Conservation Handbook*. Washington, D.C.: The Preservation Press, 1976.

"The New Sessions House." *The Building News and Engineering Journal* 91, no. 2700 (October 6, 1906).

Nylen, Robert A. "Reno's Premier Architect." *Heritage Herald* 3, no. 5 (May–June 1983).

Paher, Stanley W. *Significant County Seat Controversies in the State of Nevada*. M.A. thesis, University of Nevada, Reno, 1969.

——. *Las Vegas: As It Began—As It Grew*. Las Vegas: Nevada Publications, 1971.

——. "Courthouse on Wheels." In *Nevada Official Bicentennial Book*, edited by Stanley Paher. Las Vegas: Nevada Publications, 1976.

Patterson, Edna B., Louise A. Ulph, and Victor Goodwin. *Nevada's Northeastern Frontier*. Sparks: Western Printing and Publishing, 1969.

Pomeroy, Earl Spencer. *The Pacific Slope: A History of California, Oregon, Washington, Idaho, Utah, and Nevada*. New York: Alfred A. Knopf, 1965.

Read, Effie O. *White Pine Lang Syne*. Denver: Big Mountain Press, 1965.

Robinson, Willard B. *The People's Architecture: Texas Courthouses, Jails, and Municipal Buildings*. Austin: Texas State Historical Association, 1983.

Rowley, William D. *Reno: Hub of the Washoe County*. Woodland Hills: Windsor Publications, 1984.

Schellenberg, James A. *Conflict Between Communities: American County Seat Wars*. New York: Paragon House Publishers, 1987.

Shamberger, Hugh A. *The Story of Goldfield*. Carson City: Nevada Historical Press, 1982.

Shepperson, Wilbur S. *Mirage-Land: Images of Nevada*. Reno: University of Nevada Press, 1992.

Simmonds, Andrew. "The Blindfold of Justice." *American Bar Association Journal* 63 (September 1977).

Snider, Clyde F. *Local Government in Rural America*. New York: Appleton-Century-Crofts, 1957.

Stanyer, Jeffrey. *County Government in England and Wales*. London: Routledge Kegan Paul, 1967.

Townley, John M. *Turn this Water into Gold: The Story of the Newlands Project*. Salt Lake City: Publishers Press, 1977.

——. *Tough Little Town on the Truckee: Reno, 1868–1900*. History of Reno Series, vol. 1. Reno: Great Basin Studies Center, 1983.

Trillin, Calvin. "Temples of Democracy: The County Courthouse." *American Heritage* 28, no. 6 (October, 1977).

Venturi, Robert, Denise Scott Brown, and Steven Izenour. *Learning from Las Vegas*. Cambridge: MIT Press, 1972.

Wager, Paul W., ed. *County Government Across the Nation*. Chapel Hill: University of North Carolina Press, 1950.

Welch, June Rayfield, and Larry J. Nance. *The Texas Courthouse*. Dallas: GLA Press, 1971.

Whiffen, Marcus. *American Architecture Since*

1780: A Guide to the Styles. Cambridge: MIT Press, 1969.

Wright, Frank. "Las Vegas Hospital." National Register of Historic Places nomination, Nevada State Historic Preservation Office, Carson City, Nevada, 1987. (Removed from active register file.)

Zanjani, Sally, and Guy Louis Rocha. *The Ignoble Conspiracy: Radicalism on Trial in Nevada.* Reno: University of Nevada Press, 1986.

INDEX

Italic page numbers indicate illustrations and photographs. References to footnotes show chapter and page number.

WILBUR S. SHEPPERSON SERIES IN HISTORY AND HUMANITIES

The Nevada Constitution:
Origin and Growth (6th ed.)
Eleanore Bushnell and Don W. Driggs

His Own Counsel:
The Life and Times of Lyman Trumbull
Ralph J. Roske

Nevada's Turbulent '50s:
Decade of Political and Economic Change
Mary Ellen Glass

Henry S. Sanford: Diplomacy and Business in
Nineteenth-Century America
Joseph A. Fry

Pat McCarran: Political Boss of Nevada
Jerome E. Edwards

Servant of Power: A Political Biography
of Senator William M. Stewart
Russell R. Elliott

Austin and the Reese River Mining District:
Nevada's Forgotten Frontier
Donald R. Abbe

The Long Campaign: A Biography of Anne Martin
Anne B. Howard

The Ignoble Conspiracy:
Radicalism on Trial in Nevada
Sally Zanjani and Guy Louis Rocha

Forty Years in the Wilderness:
Impressions of Nevada, 1940–1980
James W. Hulse

The Fair But Frail:
Prostitution in San Francisco, 1849–1900
Jacqueline Baker Barnhart

American Commander in Spain: Robert Hale
Merriman and the Abraham Lincoln Brigade
Marion Merriman and Warren Lerude

Bombs in the Backyard:
Atomic Testing and American Politics
A. Costandina Titus

East of Eden, West of Zion: Essays on Nevada
edited by Wilbur S. Shepperson

The Last Resort:
Success and Failure in Campaigns for Casinos
John Dombrink and William N. Thompson

Let Justice Be Done:
Crime and Politics in Early San Francisco
Kevin J. Mullen

Resort City in the Sunbelt: Las Vegas, 1930–1970
Eugene P. Moehring

Equal to the Occasion:
Women Editors of the Nineteenth-Century West
Sherilyn Cox Bennion

The Silver State: Nevada's Heritage Reinterpreted
James W. Hulse

Mirage-Land: Images of Nevada
Wilbur S. Shepperson

The Business of Newspapers on the
Western Frontier
Barbara Cloud

George Wingfield: Owner and Operator of Nevada
C. Elizabeth Raymond

Temples of Justice: County Courthouses of Nevada
Ronald M. James